Performance Optimization *of* Numerically Intensive Codes

SOFTWARE • ENVIRONMENTS • TOOLS

The SIAM series on Software, Environments, and Tools focuses on the practical implementation of computational methods and the high performance aspects of scientific computation by emphasizing in-demand software, computing environments, and tools for computing. Software technology development issues such as current status, applications and algorithms, mathematical software, software tools, languages and compilers, computing environments, and visualization are presented.

Software, Environments, and Tools

Michael A. Heroux, Padma Raghavan, and Horst D. Simon, editors, *Parallel Processing for Scientific Computing*

Gérard Meurant, *The Lanczos and Conjugate Gradient Algorithms: From Theory to Finite Precision Computations*

Bo Einarsson, editor, *Accuracy and Reliability in Scientific Computing*

Michael W. Berry and Murray Browne, *Understanding Search Engines: Mathematical Modeling and Text Retrieval, Second Edition*

Craig C. Douglas, Gundolf Haase, and Ulrich Langer, *A Tutorial on Elliptic PDE Solvers and Their Parallelization*

Louis Komzsik, *The Lanczos Method: Evolution and Application*

Bard Ermentrout, *Simulating, Analyzing, and Animating Dynamical Systems: A Guide to XPPAUT for Researchers and Students*

V. A. Barker, L. S. Blackford, J. Dongarra, J. Du Croz, S. Hammarling, M. Marinova, J. Wasniewski, and P. Yalamov, *LAPACK95 Users' Guide*

Stefan Goedecker and Adolfy Hoisie, *Performance Optimization of Numerically Intensive Codes*

Zhaojun Bai, James Demmel, Jack Dongarra, Axel Ruhe, and Henk van der Vorst, *Templates for the Solution of Algebraic Eigenvalue Problems: A Practical Guide*

Lloyd N. Trefethen, *Spectral Methods in MATLAB*

E. Anderson, Z. Bai, C. Bischof, S. Blackford, J. Demmel, J. Dongarra, J. Du Croz, A. Greenbaum, S. Hammarling, A. McKenney, and D. Sorensen, *LAPACK Users' Guide, Third Edition*

Michael W. Berry and Murray Browne, *Understanding Search Engines: Mathematical Modeling and Text Retrieval*

Jack J. Dongarra, Iain S. Duff, Danny C. Sorensen, and Henk A. van der Vorst, *Numerical Linear Algebra for High-Performance Computers*

R. B. Lehoucq, D. C. Sorensen, and C. Yang, *ARPACK Users' Guide: Solution of Large-Scale Eigenvalue Problems with Implicitly Restarted Arnoldi Methods*

Randolph E. Bank, *PLTMG: A Software Package for Solving Elliptic Partial Differential Equations, Users' Guide 8.0*

L. S. Blackford, J. Choi, A. Cleary, E. D'Azevedo, J. Demmel, I. Dhillon, J. Dongarra, S. Hammarling, G. Henry, A. Petitet, K. Stanley, D. Walker, and R. C. Whaley, *ScaLAPACK Users' Guide*

Greg Astfalk, editor, *Applications on Advanced Architecture Computers*

Françoise Chaitin-Chatelin and Valérie Fraysse, *Lectures on Finite Precision Computations*

Roger W. Hockney, *The Science of Computer Benchmarking*

Richard Barrett, Michael Berry, Tony F. Chan, James Demmel, June Donato, Jack Dongarra, Victor Eijkhout, Roldan Pozo, Charles Romine, and Henk van der Vorst, *Templates for the Solution of Linear Systems: Building Blocks for Iterative Methods*

E. Anderson, Z. Bai, C. Bischof, J. Demmel, J. Dongarra, J. Du Croz, A. Greenbaum, S. Hammarling, A. McKenney, S. Ostrouchov, and D. Sorensen, *LAPACK Users' Guide, Second Edition*

Jack J. Dongarra, Iain S. Duff, Danny C. Sorensen, and Henk van der Vorst, *Solving Linear Systems on Vector and Shared Memory Computers*

J. J. Dongarra, J. R. Bunch, C. B. Moler, and G. W. Stewart, *Linpack Users' Guide*

Performance Optimization *of* Numerically Intensive Codes

Stefan Goedecker
Commissariat à l'énergie atomique
Grenoble, France

Adolfy Hoisie
Los Alamos National Laboratory
Los Alamos, New Mexico

Society for Industrial and Applied Mathematics
Philadelphia

Library of Congress Cataloging-in-Publication Data
Goedecker, S. (Stefan)
   Performance optimization of numerically intensive codes / Stefan Goedecker, Adolfy Hoisie.
       p. cm.--(Software, environments, tools)
   Includes bibliographical references and index.
   ISBN 978-0-898714-84-5 (pbk.)
       1. Computer architecture. 2. Electronic digital computers. 3. Parallel processing (Electronic computers). I. Title. II. Series.

QA76.9.A73 G635 2001
004.2'2–dc21   00-067939

This book was prepared as an account of work partially sponsored by an agency of the United States government. Neither the United States government nor any agency thereof, nor any of their employees, makes any warranty, express or implied, or assumes any legal liability or responsibility for the accuracy, completeness, or usefulness of any information, apparatus, product, or process disclosed, or represents that its use would not infringe privately owned rights. References herein to any specific commercial product, process, or service by trade name, trademark, manufacturer, or otherwise, does not necessarily constitute or imply its endorsement, recommendation, or favoring by the United States government or any agency thereof. The views and opinions of authors expressed herein do not necessarily state or reflect those of the United States government or any agency herein.

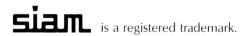 is a registered trademark.

Contents

Preface

The last decade has witnessed a tremendous increase in the amount and quality of computational science in almost all scientific disciplines. Computational science is now widely considered "at par" with the traditional theoretical and experimental components of any scientific endeavor. This extraordinary new tool in the hands of the scientist, the numerical simulation, was made possible by, and is tightly connected to, the exponential increase in the power of computers on which the computations are carried out. Modern workstations have the computational capabilities of the supercomputers of only a few years ago, while contemporary supercomputers show increases in computational capabilities of a similar magnitude. Parallel machines of various flavors provide computational resources (measured in memory), central processing unit (CPU) throughput, input/output (I/O) capabilities or network availability that allow scientists to tackle larger and larger problems with finer and finer resolution.

Whereas the computer market catering to scientific computing continues to be diverse, one can easily notice a certain convergence in the architectural design of these machines. Today, RISC (Reduced Instruction Set Computer) architectures from different vendors (Compaq/DEC, HP, IBM, SGI, SUN, etc.) are dominant. Moreover, the memory hierarchies of these architectures are quite similar. Registers, two or three levels of caches, translation look-aside buffers (TLBs), memory and disk are now present in one form or another in all architectures of practical interest. In addition, parallel computers are now built using the same off-the-shelf chips interconnected by networks of various topologies. Consequently, understanding how to achieve high performance on one architecture is of sufficient generality to allow efficient computations on almost any brand-name computer of interest.

The numerical methods underlying the computational algorithms have experienced a considerable evolution as well. As machines evolve, new and improved numerical algorithms are developed that not only solve the equations but also take better advantage of the power of the computers they run on.

The key to achieving high performance is an optimal architecture-algorithm mapping. However, the mapping of the machine architecture to algorithms is not straightforward in most cases. In a continuum spectrum, algorithmic implementations can be entirely specific to one particular architecture or developed without any insight into computer architecture, necessarily leading to poor performance.

The cost of memory traffic now dominates the cost of computing. As processors become faster and faster, the memory bandwidth needed to "feed" the processors is at a premium. This has lead to the advent of memory hierarchies that attempt to offer a way to take advantage of potentially advantageous spatial and temporal locality in the data, leading to close to peak performance. Achieving high performance on modern architectures is intimately related to a coding style that, by minimizing memory traffic, maximizes processor utilization. Otherwise, while the peak performance of workstations and parallel machines increases, the gap between peak and actual performance of codes becomes wider when no attention is paid to optimal memory utilization.

This book offers a comprehensive, tutorial-style, hands-on, introductory and intermediate-level treatment of the essential ingredients for achieving high performance in numerical computations on modern computers. We explain architectures, data traffic and issues related to performance of serial and parallel code optimization exemplified by actual programs written for algorithms of wide interest. The book is meant to bridge the gap between the literature in system architectures, the one in numerical methods and the occasional descriptions of optimization topics in computer vendors' publications.

We anticipate that the book will be of interest to any scientist, engineer or student interested in computational science and high-performance programming. We envision the book to be used as a reference book by the practitioner and as basic material for various undergraduate and graduate classes in computer and computational science.

The book is organized as follows. Chapter 2 offers a guide through basic notions of computer architectures at the level that will be utilized throughout the book. We introduce optimization techniques from the simple to the complex. Chapter 3 sets the stage by pointing out a few basic efficiency guidelines. Chapter 4 discusses timing and profiling. In Chapters 5 and 6 the all-important issues of floating point operations and memory traffic optimizations are analyzed in detail. Miscellaneous important types of optimizations are mentioned in Chapter 7, while Chapter 8 offers a very brief discussion of optimization techniques related to vector architectures. Parallel optimization is the topic of Chapter 9, where techniques and performance issues related to parallel codes are offered. Some serial and parallel case studies on problems of practical importance in scientific computing are contained in Chapter 10. Chapter 11 offers a brief overview of existing benchmarks with direct applicability to scientific computing.

The authors are indebted to many of their colleagues and friends for their contribution to the writing of this book. We would like to acknowledge the help of the following people for extremely valuable discussions, comments, technical help and critical reading of the manuscript: Hank Alme, Armin Burkhardt, Kirk Cameron, Matt Challacombe, Thierry Deutsch, Irmgard Frank, Andrew Horsfield, Jerry Huck, Jürg Hutter, Erik Koch, Matthias Krack, Olaf Lubeck, Yong Luo, Chris Mundy, Fabrizio Petrini, Anna Putrino, Karl Roessmann, Ulrich Ruede, Armin Schumacher, Yan Solihin and Harvey Wasserman. In particular we are grateful to Bill Long who invested considerable effort in reading the book and analyzing the example codes. His comments on many topics were quite helpful in improving the quality of the book.

We acknowledge the use of computational resources at the Advanced Computing Laboratory, Los Alamos National Laboratory (mainly the SGI Origin 2000), and support from the U.S. Department of Energy under contract W-7405-ENG-36. We also acknowledge access to the SP2 supercomputer at the Lawrence Livermore National Laboratory and to the Cray T3E supercomputer of the Max-Planck Rechenzentrum in Garching, Germany.

Disclaimer

This book was prepared as an account of work partially sponsored by an agency of the United States government. Neither the United States government nor any agency thereof, nor any of their employees, makes any warranty, express or implied, or assumes any legal liability or responsibility for the accuracy, completeness or usefulness of any information, apparatus, product or process disclosed, or represents that its use would not infringe privately owned rights. References herein to any specific commercial product, process or service by trade name, trademark, manufacturer or otherwise, does not necessarily constitute or imply its endorsement, recommendation or favoring by the United States government or any agency thereof. The views and opinions of authors expressed herein do not necessarily state or reflect those of the United States government or any agency herein.

Chapter 1

Introduction

The nominal peak speed, i.e., the highest theoretically attainable speed, of microprocessors is rising rapidly. This is due primarily to faster clock cycles. However, the nominal peak performance has increased at an even faster rate than the clock cycle. This additional performance gain is due mainly to an increased on-chip parallelism. Other architectural features also contribute to this, such as out-of-order execution, stream buffers, register renaming, branch prediction and speculative execution. Modern processors can now perform several operations per cycle. Future gains in performance will most likely come from a combination of improved architectural features, such as an even higher degree of on-chip parallelism, and faster clock cycles. Another important characteristic of current workstations is that memory access is very slow compared to the peak speed of the microprocessors. These trends are demonstrated in Figure 1.1 for the IBM family of Power workstation processors.

The increased on-chip parallelism, combined with the higher cost of memory traffic, leads to a drastically more difficult task in trying to achieve a significant fraction of the nominal peak speed on modern computer architectures. Even when utilizing the best possible optimization techniques, it is increasingly difficult to come close to peak performance. This is illustrated in Table 1.1, where the performance is tabulated as the percentage of peak performance for two important and highly optimized routines performing dense matrix-matrix and matrix-vector multiplication.

Yet another degree of complexity is encountered by a programmer who develops applications for parallel computers, possibly consisting of several hundred processors. Achieving 10% of the peak performance on a distributed parallel machine in a real application is usually considered an accomplishment.

In this book we will give scientists and engineers involved in numerically demanding computations the necessary knowledge to write reasonably efficient programs. The basic principles are rather simple and the possible rewards are large. Applying optimization techniques when writing code, leading to an optimal mapping of algorithms to the computer architecture, can significantly speed up a program, often by factors of 10 to 100. Optimizing a program can be a better solution than buying a faster computer!

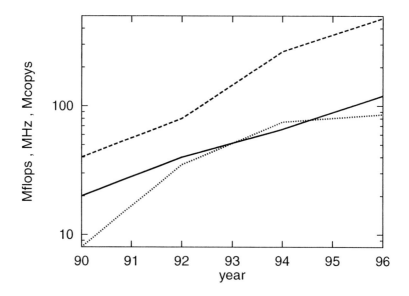

Figure 1.1: *The performance increase of IBM workstations for years 1990–1996. The solid curve shows the clock cycle (in MHz), the dashed curve the floating point peak rate (in Mflops = 10^6 floating point operations per second) and the dotted curve the main memory bandwidth (in Mcopies = 10^6 copy operations per second).*

Table 1.1: *The speed in Mflops for two standard BLAS (basic linear algebra subroutines) kernels as implemented in highly optimized vendor libraries. DGEMM does a matrix times matrix multiplication, DGEMV a matrix times vector multiplication. Both the absolute performance and its corresponding percentage of peak performance are listed. The year of the market introduction is also listed for the different workstations. 1000×1000 matrices were used in this benchmark. We presume that the DGEMV routine in the ESSL library was not optimized yet for the new Power3 architecture of the IBM 260.*

	IBM 590 (1994)	IBM 397 (1997)	IBM 260 (1999)	DEC EV6 (1999)
DGEMM	255 (97%)	545 (85%)	625 (78%)	610 (61%)
DGEMV	160 (61%)	235 (37%)	120 (15%)	535 (54%)

A relatively small number of basic optimization principles need to be applied during program development in order to obtain an efficient program. More in-depth optimization is usually needed for only a few subroutines or kernels, hence the level of effort involved is acceptable. Running an efficient program means that the time to solution is shorter for the computational problems of interest and that the available computational power is used more economically. Applying the principles and techniques described in this book is likely to boost the overall productivity of any computational scientist.

Chapter 2

Notions of Computer Architecture

The computer architectures that are at the focus of this book are "superscalar"-type architectures, characterized by on-chip instruction parallelism. All the workstations of major vendors belong to this category. A widely utilized acronym related to microprocessors is RISC (reduced instruction set computers). Most of the superscalar architectures utilize RISC instruction sets. Although not entirely equivalent, we will use the terms *RISC* and *superscalar* interchangeably in the text to describe the microprocessors with the architectural features described in this chapter. Superscalar refers only to the execution of instructions and does not constrain other architectural features. In this book we will analyze superscalar microprocessors with a hierarchical memory structure. Because of the memory hierarchy, the memory access times are not independent of the location of the data in memory. In addition to superscalar, we will briefly discuss vector architectures, which are not mainstream architectures, but have features that make them appealing for scientific computing. Finally, parallel computer architectures will be discussed.

2.1 The on-chip parallelism of superscalar architectures

Superscalar architectures can perform several operations in one cycle. An n-way superscalar processor is capable of fetching up to n instructions per cycle. Typically, a processor can perform a combination of adds, multiplies, loads/stores and branching instructions in one cycle. This instruction-level parallelism can be implemented in hardware or by a combination of hardware and software support. In hardware, a processor can have several units that work concurrently. For example, in a MIPS R10000, there are two integer units, two floating point units and one load/store unit. Thus, in each cycle, up to five instructions can be executed, one in each of the functional units listed. Instruction-level parallelism can be increased

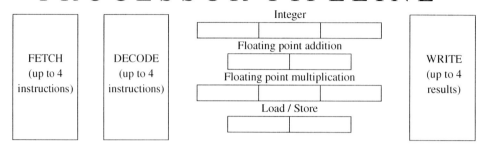

Figure 2.1: *Schematic diagram of a hypothetical four-way superscalar pipelined processor with two floating point pipelines, one integer pipeline and one load/store pipeline. The depth of these functional unit pipelines varies between two and three cycles in this processor. Consequently, the depth of the entire processor pipeline varies between five and six cycles.*

by special instructions, such as the fused multiply-add (section 5.1), that allows the execution of a floating point multiplication and a consecutive addition in one assembler instruction.

All modern processors are pipelined. Processor pipelines take advantage of the fact that all instructions can be processed in several smaller subtasks, each of which can be done within one clock cycle. The pipeline is typically subdivided into the following stages:

- Fetch instruction: Instructions are fetched from the instruction cache into the processor.

- Instruction decode and register renaming: Instructions are decoded and false dependencies are removed by register renaming.

- Issue and execute: Instructions are issued to different functional units and are executed. Some functional units, such as the floating point units, are often again pipelined. We call this "functional unit pipelining" to differentiate it from processor pipelining.

- Write back and commit: Instructions broadcast the execution result to other instructions and commit the results to the registers.

A schematic diagram of a processor of the type described in the preceding text is shown in Figure 2.1.

We note that some processors further subdivide the processor pipeline stages. For example, the Intel P6 architecture divides the decode stage into two substages, and the commit stage into three substages. The characteristics of the functional units vary from processor to processor, as is apparent from Table 2.1.

Table 2.1: *Instruction-level parallelism for several processors. The latency for dependent adds and multiplies is given in parentheses. Clock rates are quoted as of summer* 1999. *They are expected to increase in the following years. The data was obtained from analysis of publications from computer vendors and through personal contacts with their technical staff. The SUN UltraSparc* III *was announced at the time of writing.*

```
IBM RS/6000 POWERPC 604e (up to 333 MHz):
      1 floating point unit which can do
        either 1 fused multiply add (2)
                or     1 add (1)
                or     1 multiply (2)
      1 integer unit
              1 load/store
  *** 2 floating point operations per cycle (peak speed 666 Mflops)
  *** 1 memory access operation per cycle

IBM RS/6000 POWER2 (up to 160 MHz):
      2 floating point units each of which can do
        either 1 fused multiply add (2)
                or     1 add (1)
                or     1 multiply (2)
      2 integer units, each of which can do
              nearly 1 quadruple load and 1 quadruple store
              (2 adjacent real*8 numbers)
  *** 4 floating point operations per cycle (peak speed 520 Mflops)
  *** 3.5 memory access operations per cycle

IBM RS/6000 POWER3 (up to 200 MHz):
      2 floating point units each of which can do
        either 1 fused multiply add (3)
                or     1 add (3)
                or     1 multiply (3)
      2 integer units each of which can do
        either 1 address calculation or 1 fixed point operation
      1 load/store unit which can do nearly 2 loads or
        roughly 1.5 loads and 1 store
  *** 4 floating point operations per cycle (peak speed 800 Mflops)
  *** 2.5 memory access operations per cycle
  *** Out-of-order operations

Cray T3E (DEC Alpha EV5) (up to 600 MHz):
      1 floating point add pipeline (4)
      1 floating point multiply pipeline (4)
      1 load store
  *** 2 floating point operations per cycle (peak speed 1200 Mflops)
  *** 1 memory access operation per cycle

Compaq/DEC Alpha EV6 (up to 500 MHz):
      1 floating point add pipeline (4)
      1 floating point multiply pipeline (4)
      1 load
      1 store
  *** 2 floating point operations per cycle (peak speed 1000 Mflops)
  *** 2 memory access operations per cycle
  *** Out-of-order operations
```

Table 2.1: *Continued.*

```
SGI R12000/R10000 (up to 300 MHz):
      1 floating point add pipeline (2)
      1 floating point multiply pipeline (2)
      1 load store
  *** 2 floating point operations per cycle (peak speed 600 Mflops)
  *** 1 memory access operation per cycle
  *** Out-of-order operations

HP PA-RISC 8500 (up to 440 MHz):
      2 floating point units each of which can do
        either 1 fused multiply add (3)
            or    1 add (3)
            or    1 multiply (3)
      2 integer units each of which can do
        either 1 address calculation or 1 fixed point operation
      2 load/store units which can together do 2 loads or
        1 load and 1 store.
  *** 4 floating point operations per cycle (peak speed 1.6 Gflops)
  *** 2 memory access operations per cycle
  *** Out-of-order operations

SUN UltraSparc III (600 MHz):
      1 floating point add pipeline (4)
      1 floating point multiply pipeline (4)
      2 integer units
  *** 2 floating point operations per cycle (peak speed 1.2 Gflops)
  *** 2 memory access operations per cycle
```

The functional unit pipeline requires a more explicit description. This pipelining means that, besides the ability to execute different instructions in different functional units, instructions can be executed in the same functional unit simultaneously at different pipeline stages. For example, on the MIPS R10000 processor, the floating point adder and multiplier have three pipeline stages. As such, three multiplications and three additions can be processed simultaneously in each of these units when the pipeline is full, each instruction being processed in one of the three stages of the pipeline. We say in this case that the pipeline has a depth of 3. In each cycle, work on a new instruction can start in the pipeline, but it takes three cycles for its completion.

Independent instructions are processed in a pipelined functional unit such that the pipeline outputs every cycle. For dependent instructions, such as a multiplication depending on an addition $(x*(a+b))$ on the hypothetical processor in Figure 2.1, one might expect that the multiplication can only start after five cycles, the time required for the addition to propagate through the processor pipeline. Since dependencies are ubiquitous in codes, such a large latency would be detrimental to performance. In practice, though, the latency is reduced by a process called "bypassing." Through bypassing, a result available at the last stage of the functional unit pipeline can be used directly as operand of another instruction being processed in the first stage of the functional unit pipeline. In our example, the latency is reduced from five to two cycles. In other words, in the presence of bypassing, the latency of dependent operations is given by the depth of the functional unit pipeline and not by the depth of the whole processor pipeline. For a single stream of dependent operations, modern processors can typically finish a result every two to three cycles (see Table 2.1).

Special instructions, such as the fused multiply-add already mentioned under the aspect of increased parallelism, are also a means of reducing the operation's latency. In the hypothetical processor of Figure 2.1, a separate multiply-add would need five cycles for its completion, because of the dependency. For the fused multiply-add instruction, typically executed in the floating point multiplication pipeline, the latency of the instruction is reduced to three cycles. Of course, fused multiply-adds for independent instructions can output every cycle once the pipeline is filled.

Processors with out-of-order execution capabilities show less performance degradation in the presence of dependencies if several independent streams of dependent instructions can be processed. On such architectures, a queue of several instructions (e.g., 16 instructions on the R10000) waiting to be executed is maintained. Instructions for which all the operands are available are executed. The processor is dynamically switching back and forth between different streams, working only on those for which the pipeline will not stall because of missing operands.

The depth of the whole processor pipeline becomes visible as the latency of a mispredicted branch. This typically happens at the end of a loop. The program flow has to jump to a new location and start feeding the processor pipeline with a new stream of instructions. Branch prediction, found on some processors, helps to reduce the number of mispredicted branches by extrapolating the program flow pattern from data accumulated during the run.

A pipeline that cannot accept a new instruction at a certain stage is said to be "stalled." Several reasons for such stalls are possible. Two of the reasons, dependent operations and branches, were mentioned above. Other causes for stalls are due to memory access. Either the consecutive instruction is still on its way from the memory towards the processor, or, more likely, a numerical operand that has to be loaded is not yet available due to a cache miss. Keeping all the pipelines busy without stalling is one of the key ingredients for achieving high performance on RISC processors. From the point of view of the programmer, a pipeline with a latency of s cycles has practically the same effect as s separate floating point units that have a latency of just one cycle. This assertion will become clear in the discussion of the subroutine "lngth4" in section 5.2. Important characteristics of several commonly utilized processors are summarized in Table 2.1. Information on a much wider range of processors can be found at http://infopad.EECS.Berkeley.EDU/CIC/summary/local/.

2.2 Overview of the memory hierarchy of RISC architectures

The memory subsystem of RISC computers is organized hierarchically. It can be visualized as a layered inverted pyramid [12]. Layers at the top are big but have slow access times. Layers towards the bottom of the pyramid are small but have fast access times since they are close to the central processing unit (CPU). The size of the data packets transferred among the different layers varies as well. Data movement between the layers at the top involves larger amounts of data. The chunks of data transferred decrease to as little as one word at the bottom of the memory hierarchy. We will now describe this reversed pyramid in more detail, starting at the bottom with the smallest layer.

The fastest but smallest memory level is composed of the registers, placed on the chip, housing the CPU. All high-end RISC processors have 32 floating point logical registers that can be accessed without any delay (0-cycle latency). Pentium-based machines have many fewer registers, 8 at most on the Pentium III. On some machines, not all of these 32 registers are accessible to program operands. Some of the registers are reserved for special purposes. In addition to the floating point registers, there are also typically 32 integer registers. They are used for integer arithmetic, including the calculation of the addresses of array elements that are loaded or stored. In this context it is worthwhile pointing out that the number of physical registers can be larger than the number of logical registers. This allows for register renaming, a process that will be explained in more detail in section 5.5.

The next level in the memory hierarchy is the cache. Many machines have multiple cache levels, a level-1 (L1) cache and a level-2 (L2) cache, for example. An L1 cache can usually be accessed with a one-cycle latency if the data is available in the cache. Since in many cases a load or store from the L1 cache to a register can be overlapped with floating point operations, this one-cycle latency can often be hidden, giving the appearance of a zero-cycle access time. Data transfer from the L1 cache to the registers takes place in units of words (i.e., single or double precision numbers). If the data is not in the L1 level, it has to be fetched from the higher level of the memory hierarchy, the memory or the L2 cache. A "cache miss" occurs and the program execution has to wait for several cycles until the data are transferred into the L1 cache. In the same way, an L2 cache miss can occur, necessitating a data transfer from the main memory. The penalty for an L2 cache miss is larger than for an L1 cache miss. The penalty is typically in the range of a few dozen cycles for an L1 miss, and as high as 100 cycles for an L2 miss. The smallest possible unit that can be loaded from memory into the cache is a cache line, typically comprising between 4 and 32 words. The cache line sizes for the various cache levels can be different. The memory hierarchy of an IBM 590 workstation is shown in Figure 2.2.

At this point it is important to note that although we will be concentrating in this book on data caches, L1 instruction caches are also present. The goals of the instruction cache are very similar to those of the data cache, only applied to instructions. Frequently used instructions are accommodated closer to the CPU in order to achieve faster access times. If two cache levels exist, then typically the second-level cache is used for both data and instructions.

The next generic hierarchy level is the memory attached to one processor. The slow access time (high latency) of the CPU to data in the main memory is a major bottleneck in many scientific applications. Another, equally important bottleneck is the limited memory bandwidth, i.e., the limited amount of data that can be

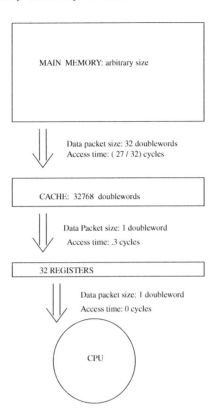

Figure 2.2: *Schematic view of the memory hierarchy of an IBM 590 workstation.*

transferred from the memory towards the lower levels of the memory hierarchy. One architectural technique leading to an increased memory bandwidth is memory interleaving. As an example, an IBM 590 workstation has four memory banks. If a cache line, 32 words in size, is brought into cache from memory, then the first 8 words are filled from the first memory bank, the second 8 words from the second bank, and so on. The memory bandwidth is increased four times compared to the case of a single memory bank. However, memory interleaving has no beneficial effect on the latency. If only a single word of the 32 words of a cache line is needed, the memory access time is latency bound and would not benefit from memory interleaving. Data access with stride 1 is therefore faster compared with larger stride access.

In the case of a distributed memory parallel computer, one more memory level is added, the global memory comprising all of the local memories of the individual processors. Access to remote memories is generally done via communication libraries over the interconnect network, as will be detailed in section 2.8. Such data transfers usually involve high latency and small bandwidth compared to in-processor data transfers.

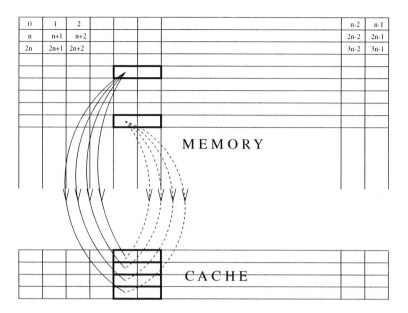

Figure 2.3: *Mapping rules for a four-way associative cache. Each memory location can be mapped to four cache locations, but many memory locations map to the same four cache locations. Since we assumed that the cache line size is two words, the portion to be transferred is the framed area.*

2.3   Mapping rules for caches

In a fully associative cache, a cache line can be placed in any free slot in the cache. Fully associative caches are rarely used for data caches, but are sometimes for translation look-aside buffers (TLBs) (see section 2.5). In the standard non-fully associative cache, a cache line that is loaded from the main memory can only be placed in a limited number of locations in the cache. Based on the number of such possible locations, we distinguish between directly and indirectly mapped caches. In a directly mapped cache, there is only one possible location. Indirectly mapped caches allow for more than one location.

If the size of the cache is n words, then the ith word in memory can be stored only in the position given by $\mathrm{mod}(i, n)$ in directly mapped caches. If we have an m_{as}-way associative cache of size $m_{as} \times n$, then any location in memory can be mapped to m_{as} possible locations in cache, given by the formula $j \times n + \mathrm{mod}(i, n)$, where $j = 0, \ldots, m_{as} - 1$. The situation for a four-way associative cache with a cache line size of two words is illustrated in Figure 2.3.

If, in an m_{as}-way associative cache, all the m_{as} possible locations for a data set are taken, one of them has to be overwritten. On most processors, the least recently used entry will be overwritten. On the three-way associative L2 cache of a Cray T3E, the entry to be overwritten is chosen at random.

In relation to the way in which the data from the cache is written back to memory, we distinguish write-through and write-back caches. In a write-through cache, each element that is stored is immediately updated in the memory. In this case, each store involves a memory access. In a write-back cache, the stores are written back to the cache. The cache line containing the store gets updated into the main memory only when the space in cache is needed for another cache line. When this occurs, two memory accesses are needed: the write back of the old cache line, followed by the cache loading of the new line. A "dirty bit" attached to each cache line identifies the cache lines of a write-back cache requiring a backup into memory before they can be overwritten. When an element of a cache line is modified, the dirty bit is set, indicating that the cache line needs to be written back to memory before it is replaced in the cache.

These considerations make it apparent that stores are costlier than loads for both write-through and write-back caches. Loads are handled in the same way by both types of caches. Memory access is required whenever a word that is not part of a cache-resident cache line is accessed.

2.4   A taxonomy of cache misses

Cache misses can be categorized as follows [24]:

- Compulsory cache misses: These misses occur when the cache line has to be brought into the cache when first accessing it. They are unavoidable.

- Capacity cache misses: They are related to the limited size of the cache preventing all the necessary data to be in the cache simultaneously. New data brought into the cache may have to overwrite older entries.

- Conflict cache misses: These misses occur in directly mapped or set associative caches. Because of the mapping rules, the effective cache size is usually smaller than the physical cache size. The effective cache size would be equal to the physical cache size only if a data item from the main memory could go into any location in the cache. Since this is not the case, unoccupied cache line slots will frequently be found in the cache, thus reducing the effective cache size. The extreme case, when most of the physical cache space is not available because of these mapping rules, is called cache thrashing.

Different types of caches behave differently under cache misses. A blocking cache will stop servicing further requests upon a cache miss until the cache line is stored in the cache, whereas a nonblocking cache will proceed working under the same conditions.

Programming techniques leading to a reduction of the number of cache misses will be discussed throughout the book.

2.5   TLB misses

RISC workstations are virtual memory machines. This means that they distinguish between a logical and a physical memory address. The logical address is the one utilized in a program to identify array elements. The array elements x(100) and x(600) have the logical address of 100 and 600, respectively. However, they are not necessarily at the physical locations 100 and 600 in the memory. Logical addresses are translated into physical ones as described below.

Each address belongs to a page in the memory. The size of a memory page varies from machine to machine. For example, on the IBM 590 one page holds 2^9 = 512 doublewords (one doubleword = 8 bytes). In this case, the array element x(100) would be on the first logical page, while x(600) would belong to the second logical page. A page can be stored in any physical page slot in memory or even on disk.

A page table, stored in the main memory, keeps track of the mapping from physical to logical addresses. The most frequently used entries of that table are stored in a special cache, the TLB. Thus, when accessing a logical memory location that belongs to a logical page whose mapping to a physical address is not present in the TLB, that page location has to be fetched from the much larger page table. A TLB miss will occur, very similar to a cache miss for all practical purposes, only costlier.

From the point of view of the programmer, the effect of a TLB is exactly the same as if there were an extra cache level whose cache line size is equal to the page size and whose overall size is equal to the total number of words contained in all the pages whose physical addresses can be held in the TLB. For optimal performance, any data item has to be contained in both memory hierarchy levels. In other words, both the capacity misses and the conflict misses have to be minimized not only for the real cache levels but also for the TLB level. On an IBM 590, the TLB is a two-way associative cache with 2×256 entries each holding 512 doublewords. Its effect is therefore the same as an additional two-way associative cache level with a total capacity of 2^{18} words and a cache line length of 512. The TLB and the data caches are accessed in parallel. Thus, in the event of a combined cache and a TLB miss, the latency is smaller than the sum of the individual latencies.

2.6   Multilevel cache configurations

Most of the modern RISC computers have two or even three cache levels. The reason for this lies in the tradeoffs that a computer architect has to make in order to achieve a balanced, high-performance architecture. An L1 cache is usually built on-chip. Given the limitations on the number of transistors on a chip and the high cost of a cache in terms of transistor consumption, a tradeoff is made between the size of the cache and the features and complexity of the CPU. For these on-chip "real-estate" reasons, the larger L2 caches are built off-chip. Because of the longer signal traveling time, off-chip caches are slower in access time, but they can

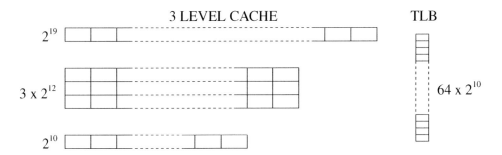

Figure 2.4: *The memory hierarchy of a Digital* AU433 *workstation consisting of a* L3 *cache with a capacity of* 2^{19} *doublewords, a three-way associative* L2 *cache with a capacity of* 3×2^{12}, *and an* L1 *cache with a capacity of* 2^{10}. *The* TLB *is fully associative and can hold* 64 *pages of* 2^{10} *doublewords each.*

be significantly larger than the L1 caches. Figure 2.4 shows the three-level cache hierarchy of a Digital AU433 workstation.

The behavior of such a multilevel cache structure is quite complex [21], as it depends not only on the sizes and associativity sets, but also on whether the cache structure is inclusive or exclusive. In an inclusive cache structure, each level has to hold its own copy of the same cache line. In an exclusive cache structure only one copy is shared among the different cache levels. As mentioned before, a TLB can be considered as an inclusive cache.

2.7   Characteristics of memory hierarchies on some common machines

Table 2.2 gives an overview of important memory hierarchy parameters for a few architectures of commercial interest.

2.8   Parallel architectures

2.8.1   Shared memory architectures

Parallel computers [11] are classified according to how the memory is laid out. In shared memory machines, all the processors have access to a unique global memory. They are also known as symmetric multiprocessors (SMPs). In older designs of this type of computer, the processors were connected via a single bus system to the global memory. This leads to contention among the processors for the available bandwidth of the shared bus. The more processors there are competing for memory access, the slower the memory access for each processor becomes. As a consequence, the maximum number of processors that can be used in such an architecture is rather small, on the order of 8 processors. In newer SMP models, the bus system is replaced by a crossbar switch. The processors can simultaneously exchange data

Table 2.2: *The characteristics of the different levels of the memory hierarchy of several RISC computers. Sizes are always given as a product, where the first term is the associativity of the level. If the second term of the product is 1, the level is fully associative. The units are doublewords (8 bytes). Since a TLB behaves essentially like a cache, the TLB size is denoted by "ncache_size" and the page size by "ncache_line." The data were obtained in the same way as those in Table 2.1. This information was compiled from vendor literature and architecture designers.*

```
IBM POWER PC 604e (233 MHz)
    1. LEVEL: L1 cache:
            ncache_size= 4 X 1024
            ncache_line= 8
            write through, least recently used replacement policy
    2. LEVEL: TLB:
            ncache_size= 2 X 32768
            ncache_line= 512


IBM RS/6000 POWER2 model 590 (66 MHz):
    1. LEVEL: L1 cache:
            ncache_size= 4 X 8192
            ncache_line= 32
            write back, least recently used replacement policy
    2. LEVEL: TLB:
            ncache_size= 2 X 131072
            ncache_line= 512


IBM RS/6000 POWER2 model 397 (160 MHz):
    1. LEVEL: L1 cache:
            ncache_size= 4 X 4096
            ncache_line= 32
            nonblocking, write back, least recently used replacement policy
    2. LEVEL: TLB:
            ncache_size= 2 X 65536
            ncache_line= 512


IBM RS/6000 POWER3 model 260 (200 MHz):
    1. LEVEL: L1 cache:
            ncache_size= 128 X 64
            ncache_line= 16
            nonblocking, write back, robin round, fourfold interleaved
            can be fed by prefetching directly from memory
    2. LEVEL: TLB:
            ncache_size= 2 X 65536
            ncache_line= 512
    3. LEVEL: L2 cache:
            ncache_size= 1 X 524288
            ncache_line= 16
            noninclusive


Cray T3E (DEC Alpha EV5) (up to 600 MHz):
    1. LEVEL: L1 cache:
            ncache_size= 1 X 1024
            ncache_line= 4
            write through
```

Table 2.2: *Continued.*

```
        2. LEVEL: L2 cache
                   ncache_size= 3 X 2048
                   ncache_line= 8
                   write back
        3. LEVEL: TLB:
                   ncache_size= 65536 X 1
                   ncache_line= 1024

Compaq/DEC Alpha EV6 (up to 500 MHz):
        1. LEVEL: L1 cache:
                   ncache_size= 2 X 4096
                   ncache_line= 4
                   pseudowrite back
        2. LEVEL: L2 cache
                   ncache_size= up to 1 X 524288 (up to 16 Mbytes)
                   ncache_line= 8
                   nearly write back
        3. LEVEL: TLB:
                   ncache_size= 131072 X 1
                   ncache_line= 1024

SGI R12000/R10000 ( up to 300 MHz):
        1. LEVEL: L1 cache:
                   ncache_size= 2 X 2048
                   ncache_line= 4
                   write back, least recently used replacement policy,
                   twofold interleaved
        2. LEVEL: L2 cache:
                   ncache_size= up to 2 X 524288 (8 Mbytes)
                   ncache_line= 16
                   write back
        3. LEVEL: TLB:
                   ncache_size= 32768 X 1
                   ncache_line= 512

HP PA-RISC 8500 (up to 440 MHz):
        1. LEVEL: L1 cache:
                   ncache_size= 4 X 32768
                   ncache_line= 8
                   nonblocking, write back, pseudo-LRU, with
                   multiple-outstanding-request queue
        2. LEVEL: TLB
                   120 entries, fully associative
                   variable page sizes from 4KB to 64MB

SUN UltraSparc III (600 MHz):
        1. LEVEL: L1 cache:
                   ncache_size= 4 X 2048
                   ncache_line= 16
                   write through
        2. LEVEL: L2 cache:
                   ncache_size= up to 1 X 1048576 (8 Mbytes)
                   ncache_line=512 (for the 8 Mbytes size)
                   noninclusive
                   hardware prefetching
```

with each other as well as with the memory. Even in this case, the maximum number of processors is limited. First, it is difficult and expensive to construct crossbars that connect a large number of elements. Second, the overall rate at which data can be extracted out of a single memory is limited for a given number of memory banks. Thus, crossbar-connected RISC SMP machines typically consist of no more than 8 processors. High-end vector SMPs go up to 32 processors.

Most RISC-based SMPs enforce cache coherence at a cache line level. Maintaining the coherence and consistency of the data is a major performance problem. As an example, data that is loaded into the cache of a processor can be modified by it. To prevent another processor from using invalid data, any cache line that is loaded into the cache of a processor has to be tagged as reserved on the other processors. Cache coherence protocols involve a substantial overhead. If several processors access data on a single cache line, they have to compete for the ownership of that cache line. In this worst-case scenario, the parallel performance of several SMP processors will be lower than the serial performance of a single processor.

Traditional vector processors do not have a cache, hence the problem of cache coherence does not exist on vector SMPs.

On the Cray SV1, a vector machine with a cache, cache coherence is not enforced. A parallel job synchronizes at the beginning and the end of regions of the program that are executed in parallel, by using test-and-set instructions on special hardware registers. Test-and-set instructions have the side effect of flushing the cache. In this scheme, a significant overhead is paid when entering a parallel region, but no performance degradation occurs in the parallel region itself. This technique is efficient when the amount of work in the parallel region is sufficiently large.

The parallelization for SMPs done automatically by the compiler is not optimal [20], in general. The compiler has a particularly difficult job on machines that enforce cache coherence since it should generate machine code that minimizes cache contention. Performance optimization for SMP machines involves manually inserting compiler directives that are vendor specific. Therefore, programs are not easily portable to machines from different vendors. The new OpenMP (http://www.openmp.org) standard that has been adopted by the major SMP vendors may change the situation from that point of view. One possibility of insuring portability on SMPs is the usage of message passing (see section 2.8.2), in spite of the fact that it is somewhat contrary to the spirit of such an architecture. Since some data sharing overhead can be eliminated in this way on cache-coherent SMPs, performance of MPI-based codes can be very good.

On high-end vector SMP machines, in particular from Cray, microtasking with compiler directives leads to best performance levels.

2.8.2 Distributed memory architectures

For large-scale parallel scientific calculations, for which the run time must be many times smaller than that on a single processor, large-scale distributed memory computers, also known as massively parallel processors (MPPs) are the platform of choice. We will concentrate in this book on this type of architecture.

The global memory of such machines consists of all the local memories distributed among the individual processors. MPPs are best characterized by the topology of the network connecting the processors. Interconnection networks are classified in two main categories: direct and indirect networks. In "direct" networks [22], point-to-point links interconnect the nodes in a fixed topology. Examples of such topologies available in commercially important MPPs include the hypercube and the three-dimensional torus. An "indirect" network [26] is a switch-based interconnection. This class of networks allows the interconnection pattern to be varied dynamically. Hence, in indirect networks, connections can be established between any two processors. Examples of such networks include crossbars, buses and multistage networks. Such networks are well suited for the communication requirements of most applications, since many of the communication patterns generated by these applications can be embedded in an indirect network architecture with low contention.

In MPPs, processors exchange data by using message passing over the interconnection network. The exchange is handled by communication libraries that have to be called from within the program. In contrast to a shared memory machine, the programmer is solely responsible for the distribution of the data among the processors and their correct communication through message passing calls.

The efficiency of the message passing paradigm depends on many factors such as the network topology, the characteristics of the links between processors in such a network and the software protocols governing the data traffic. Let us start with a discussion of some basic concepts in point-to-point communication, i.e., a communication involving only one pair of processors.

Two main performance numbers are associated with point-to-point communication, the latency and the bandwidth. By definition the latency is the time needed to send a zero-length message from one node to another. Alternatively, the latency can be interpreted as the start-up cost for a message. Bandwidth is usually quoted as the maximum speed of message transfer in Mbytes/second for an infinitely large message. The effective bandwidth (i.e., the bandwidth measured for a finite length message) involves the latency and is therefore message size dependent. A typical curve of the effective bandwidth vs. message size is presented in Figure 2.5.

By using these two parameters, we can express the time T for sending a message as

$$T = L + M/B, \tag{2.1}$$

where L is the latency, M is the size of the message and B is the bandwidth. It is apparent that for communication patterns involving short messages latency is the dominant factor in T. Large messages are bandwidth dominated. An important point is that, given the complexity of the protocols utilized in communication libraries, it is unlikely that a single pair (latency, bandwidth) can describe the whole range of message sizes and all communication libraries. Latency is in the range of a few microseconds to low tens of microseconds on the most utilized parallel architectures. On the Cray T3E, the latency is one microsecond for a direct memory access mechanism ("SHMEM") but of the order of 10 to 20 microseconds for communication using MPI, see section 8.2. The effective bandwidth on most current parallel

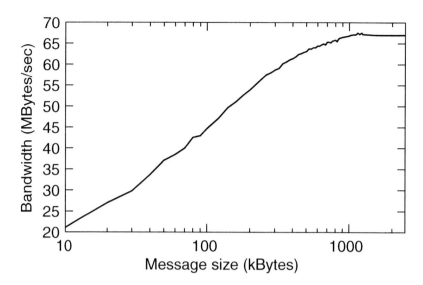

Figure 2.5: *The effective point-to-point bandwidth as a function of the message size on a CRAY T3E. The MPI_SENDRECV routine was used for this measurement.*

machines ranges from about 100 Mbytes per second on the SGI Origin 2000 to 300 Mbytes per second on the Cray T3E and the IBM SP3.

Many basic message passing communication patterns involve not only point-to-point communications, but also "global" communications, where all (or groups of) processors are simultaneously involved in data exchanges. An example of such a communication pattern is a global data transposition visualized in Figure 2.6.

For global communications, the "bisectional bandwidth" is a good performance indicator. The bisectional bandwidth is the total bandwidth from one half of the machine to the other half if the network is cut by an imaginary plane into two halves. Consequently, it is equal to the total number of links traversing this plane times the point-to-point bandwidth. The bisectional bandwidth depends strongly on the topology of the parallel computer, as will be explained in the following when presenting the most widely utilized topologies.

In a hypercube topology the processors are on the corners of a d-dimensional cube and the communication links are the edges connecting the corners. For a given d, the number of processors is 2^d and the number of communication links cutting through any dividing plane is 2^{d-1}. Hence, the bisectional bandwidth grows linearly with the number of processors. Hypercubes of up to dimension 4 are shown in Figure 2.7. Higher dimensional hypercubes are difficult to visualize.

Even though the bisectional bandwidth scales linearly with the number of processors, communication becomes more expensive for larger dimensions, since a message has to travel through d links between the farthest placed processors. This means that, in such cases, the latency can grow logarithmically with respect to the number of processors. The SGI Origin2000 computer is an example of a hypercube architecture. However, there are two important modifications to the ideal hyper-

$\mathbf{P_0}$	$\mathbf{P_1}$	$\mathbf{P_2}$	$\mathbf{P_3}$
1,1	1,2	1,3	1,4
2,1	2,2	2,3	2,4
3,1	3,2	3,3	3,4
4,1	4,2	4,3	4,4

$\mathbf{P_0}$	$\mathbf{P_1}$	$\mathbf{P_2}$	$\mathbf{P_3}$
1,1	2,1	3,1	4,1
1,2	2,2	3,2	4,2
1,3	2,3	3,3	4,3
1,4	2,4	3,4	4,4

Figure 2.6: *The distribution of data among processors before (left-hand side) and after (right-hand side) a global data transposition on four processors. Each processor has to communicate with all the other processors. For simplicity, we assume here that only a single element of this four-by-four matrix is exchanged between any two processors.*

cube concept in the Origin 2000 topology. First, each corner has two nodes and each node has two processors. Second, for configurations in more than five dimensions, some of the links that would be found in a true hypercube are missing. Thus, the bisectional bandwidth no longer scales linearly with the number of processors for large configurations. The specific variant of the Origin 2000 topology is known as a fat-bristled hypercube.

Other important topologies are the d-dimensional meshes and toruses. The only difference between a mesh and a torus is that in a torus the processors on the surfaces are connected with the processors on the opposite surfaces. This is shown for the two-dimensional case in Figure 2.8.

In a mesh or a torus the bisectional bandwidth does not increase linearly with the number of processors. In a three-dimensional torus with side length l, for example, the number of processors grows as l^3, but the bisectional bandwidth only as l^2. The Cray T3E is an example of a parallel machine with a three-dimensional torus network topology.

A parallel computer with an indirect network is the IBM SP2. As was already mentioned, in an indirect network any processor can dynamically be connected to any other processor, with the implication that a parallel program does not need to be executed on a team of processors that are topologically close for best performance. Ignoring possible network congestion, any random collection of processors can be selected. As an aside, for a buyer with limited resources, a computer with a switch-based network has the advantage that it can be purchased with any number of processors and not only with certain magic processor numbers that correspond to a full topological configuration.

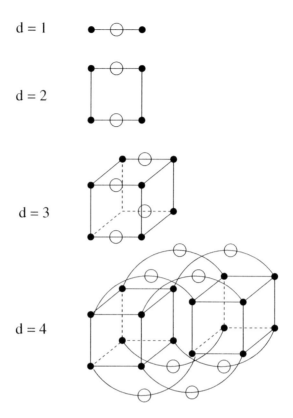

Figure 2.7: *Hypercube topologies for the cases d = 1, 2, 3, and 4. The processors are indicated by the filled dots, the communication links by lines and the crossings of these links by an imaginary plane cutting the hypercube into two halves by empty circles. The number of empty circles is always half the number of the filled dots. Hence, the bisectional bandwidth is proportional to the number of processors.*

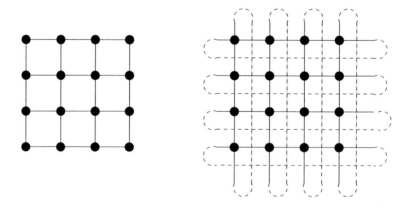

Figure 2.8: *A two-dimensional mesh (right) and torus (left).*

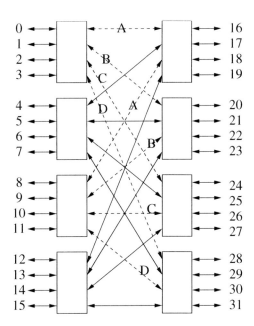

Figure 2.9: *The IBM SP2 multistage switch for a 32-processor configuration. The crossbars are denoted by squares with four input and four output links. The switch is laid out in such a way that there is always a four-way redundancy for any point-to-point communication path. The four possible paths between any pair of processors in the groups 0 to 3 and 8 to 11 are indicated by the dashed lines A, B, C, D.*

The SP2 switch [4] is built as a hierarchy of stages based on four-by-four cross-bar switches. As was already mentioned, a crossbar is a device that allows several arbitrary pairs of input and output ports (four pairs in this case) to communicate simultaneously with each other. The layout of the switch for a 32-processor configuration is shown in Figure 2.9. The switch is designed such that the bisectional bandwidth scales linearly with the number of processors, as in the case of a hypercube. Since one additional level in the hierarchy is needed whenever the number of processors is doubled, the hardware latency will increase logarithmically with the number of processors. Such topological effects of the switch are not visible to the user on the SP2, since total latencies are dominated by software and not by hardware latencies.

In practice, the latency and bisectional bandwidth on all these machines is much more influenced by the quality of the communication library than by these fundamental topology considerations. The trends that one would expect to see based on topology reasoning are completely masked by software overheads. Figure 2.10 shows timings for a global data transposition on several major parallel computers. From our theoretical consideration, one would expect the Cray T3E performance to deteriorate considerably for large configurations. However, Figure 2.10 shows that this is not the case, at least for configurations up to 128 processors. As a matter of fact, the Cray T3E exhibits the fastest global communication in this processor range.

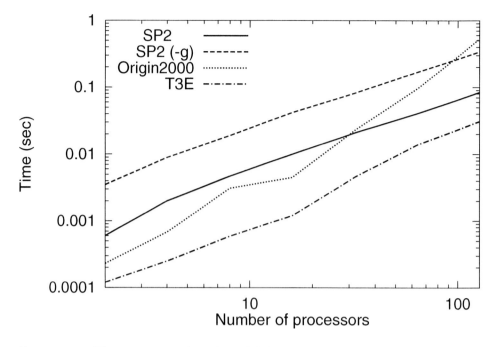

Figure 2.10: *The time required to do a global data transposition using the message passing interface (MPI; see section 8.2) ALLTOALL routine. The data size is* 1000 *doublewords. Data are shown for the Cray T3E, SGI Origin2000 and the IBM SP2. Each node of the IBM SP2 is an SMP containing four PowerPC nodes (model 604). Without the "−g" option, only one processor per node is used; the remaining three are idle. With the "−g" option, all four processors in a node are utilized. They all have to compete for a single port to the network, leading to lower performance. From the point of view of bisectional bandwidth, MPPs have an edge over clusters of SMPs.*

Clusters of workstations are another example of parallel distributed memory configurations. Their communication network is in general considerably slower than the special-purpose network of massively parallel supercomputers. Nevertheless, clusters are popular because of their advantageous price/performance ratio. (See, for example, http://cnls.lanl.gov:80/avalon/.)

2.8.3   Distributed shared memory architectures

We initially classified parallel computers in shared and distributed memory machines. Recently, these two apparently mutually exclusive architectures have been merged with the advent of distributed shared memory (DSMs) architectures. In DSMs the memory is physically distributed among processors. A shared view of the global memory is provided, typically by a combination of hardware and software techniques. In principle, DSMs should make programming easier, since explicit message passing is not needed. However, the overhead to be paid for this convenience is costly in terms of performance. Cache coherence in DSMs is even more expensive than in the case of SMPs. The SGI Origin 2000 is an example of a DSM architecture. In order to achieve the highest possible level of performance, we had to use message passing with MPI on the SGI Origin for all the programs presented later in the book.

A different breed of supercomputers that does not fit straightforwardly into the shared/distributed memory scheme are the clusters of SMPs. This architecture makes performance programming very complex, unless at least one level of parallelism (most likely the SMP level) is satisfactorily achieved by the compiler. The new IBM SP3 series, or clusters of Origin 2000s in existence at various sites, are examples of such architectures. The test programs we run on SMP-based SP2s all ignored the SMP character of a node, assuming that each processor behaves as if it formed a node by itself.

2.9   A comparison between vector and superscalar architectures

Even though RISC architectures with hierarchical memory structures are at the center of interest in this book, we will briefly digress to discuss some concepts related to vector machines [23].

Vector architectures were designed to maximize floating point performance only. This is a different design philosophy from RISC architectures, which are designed as general-purpose processors. This implies that, besides floating point intensive codes pervasive in scientific computing, the requirements of integer arithmetic–bound applications permeated the design of modern superscalar. Example of drivers for the design of new architectures are data mining, multimedia and web applications. Hence RISC processors' design represents a compromise between the often conflicting requirements of different applications.

A main difference between RISC and vector computers is the faster memory access time on the latter, resulting from a more sophisticated memory structure. The cycle time of the CPU is practically the same nowadays for both vector supercomputers and high-end superscalar processors. There are also architectural similarities. As a matter of fact, several ideas that were pioneered some 20 years ago in the early vector machines, such as CPU pipelines and bypassing, described in section 2.1, can now also be found in superscalar processors.

In addition to scalar instructions, vector machines have "vector instructions" that apply identical instructions to multiple data. The vector length specifies how many data or groups of data the instruction is applied to. As an example, a vector addition of length 64 will calculate 64 elements of the sum vector by adding 64 pairs of elements of the two input vectors. The fact that we call data sets "vectors" does not imply that they correspond to one-dimensional arrays of the same length in the program. In most cases the arrays in the program will have larger dimensions and the vectors will be subsets of these arrays. These subsets need not even be contiguous.

The functional unit of a vector machine is deeply pipelined, for instance, nine stages on the latest Cray SV1. Bypassing, actually called chaining on vector machines, is also present. On the SV1, this means that the first result of a vector instruction is available as an input for a subsequent vector instruction after nine cycles. Since one result is finished in each cycle, the last result of a vector instruction of length 64 will be available after 73 cycles for chaining.

The size of the vector registers determines the maximal vector length. It is typically 64, 128, or 256. On a machine with a vector length of 64, a very long loop will be chopped into pieces of 64 and a remainder with a shorter vector length. The number of vector registers is much smaller than the number of scalar registers on a RISC architecture. On most Cray machines there are eight vector registers. Latency of a vector register load can be hidden by overlapping vector loads with execution of data contained in other vector registers. This latency hiding is much more efficient on vector than on RISC machines, as the number of cycles for graduating the content of a vector register is much larger than for a scalar register on a RISC machine, roughly 64 cycles compared to 1 cycle. Prefetching is utilized on RISC machines (see section 6.11) to obtain a similar effect.

In addition to vector pipelines, vector machines have scalar floating point units. These units deal with short loops, where vector instructions would lead to low performance, as well as with loops that are "nonvectorizable" because of their structure. For example, nonremovable dependencies in recursive loops as well as some conditional branches inhibit vectorization.

When working on small data sets that fit in cache, a relatively cheap workstation can be as fast as an expensive vector supercomputer. The workstation may actually be faster on very short inner loops or on nonvectorizable code. On the other hand, when working on large data sets that are not cache resident and on inner loops large enough for efficient vectorization, the vector computer is likely to surpass the workstation in performance. In contrast to a superscalar processor, the vector processor can feed the CPU fast enough with the required data due to its memory latency hiding mechanism and high bandwidth.

The reason why the bandwidth is much larger on vector machines is that its memory is organized into a very large number of memory banks. As we have already seen when we analyzed the memory bandwidth in the context of superscalar architectures in section 2.2, an interleaved memory leads to a higher bandwidth. The reasoning is similar for vector machines. After being accessed, a memory bank needs a "refresh time" to recover, during which it cannot serve further data requests. If data is fetched from other banks during this relatively long refresh time, the delays can overlap and the bandwidth increases. On workstations, the interleaved memory increases the bandwidth only for short stride data access, since consecutive memory banks are used to fill a single cache line. If the stride is larger than the length of a cache line, then the increased bandwidth is wasted, as the data in that cache line coming from different memory banks are never used. Vector machines are more flexible from this point of view. The data originating from the different banks are used to fill a vector register, and the different slots in this vector register need not refer to items that are adjacent in memory. Thus, high bandwidth for nonunit stride memory access can be achieved. For certain scientific and engineering applications, in which large regions of memory are traversed with nonunit stride, vector machines are therefore significantly faster than the fastest RISC workstations.

The performance advantages of vector machines are equally important in gather- $(y(i) = x(ind(i)))$ and scatter- $(y(ind(i)) = x(i))$ type loops involving indirect addressing. Special vector hardware gives high performance in computations of this type.

The SV1 vector processor from Cray aims at reconciling the advantages of RISC architectures, including low cost, with the advantages of vector processors for some numerically intensive applications. Its memory consists of a very large number of memory banks (up to 1024) made out of standard DRAM, slower but cheaper than the SRAM typically used in vector systems. Another difference from traditional vector machine design is that a cache of 32K words is added to hide memory latencies.

Chapter 3

A Few Basic Efficiency Guidelines

In this chapter we will not dive deeply into sophisticated optimization techniques. Rather we will propose some basic efficiency guidelines that can improve program performance without any significant time investment by the programmer.

3.1 Selection of best algorithm

Usually several algorithms are available for a specific problem. Choosing the algorithm that is best suited for the problem of interest and the target computer clearly is the first and most important step. Frequently, the complexity or scaling behavior of two algorithms is different. For instance, the number of operations in a matrix-matrix multiplication is N^3 for $N \times N$ matrices with the ordinary algorithm, but only $N^{2.8}$ with the Strassen algorithm [25]. For large data sets, the advantage of using a low-complexity algorithm (the Strassen algorithm in the matrix multiplication example) is overwhelming and certainly dominates other suitability aspects. If, under such circumstances, the implementation of a low-complexity algorithm is not well adapted to the computer architecture, the advantages of using it could be lost. The common sense solution is to find a better implementation of this algorithm instead of using a potentially high-performance implementation of the higher complexity algorithm. In a different situation, if two algorithms differ in their operation count by only a small factor, the potential for a good implementation on a specific architecture may be the dominating aspect. This book will present the information necessary to judge the suitability of different algorithms for various architectures.

3.2 Use of efficient libraries

High-quality numerical libraries are available for most of the basic computational problems. Instead of duplicating work by developing and optimizing one's own version, one should definitely use such library routines whenever available.

Table 3.1: *Comparison of the speed of different levels of BLAS routines on an IBM 590 workstation with a peak speed of 265 Mflops. A matrix-matrix multiplication is done by calls to different BLAS levels. In this example, Level-1 BLAS has nonunit stride and, for comparison, the performance for unit stride is given as well. The BLAS subroutines utilized are part of the IBM ESSL library.*

BLAS routine	Speed (Mflops)
DGEMM (Level-33: matrix matrix mult.)	255
DGEMV (Level-22: matrix vector mult.)	160
DDOT (Level-1: scalar product)	4
DDOT (scalar product, unit stride)	110

For most basic dense linear algebra computations, the BLAS (basic linear algebra subroutines; http://www.netlib.org/index.html) is a highly recommended library, particularly when provided in optimized form by computer vendors for their specific architecture. Optimized BLAS routines can be found in the ESSL library for the IBM machines, in the DXML library for the Compaqs, in the SCSL library for SGIs and in the LIBSCI for Crays. Since the calling sequence is the same in all vendor-optimized implementations, a program using BLAS routines is portable to any computer.

There are three levels of BLAS. Level-1 contains vector–vector kernels, such as a scalar product between two vectors, level-2 deals with matrix–vector operations, such as matrix times vector multiplication, and level-3 contains matrix–matrix routines, such as matrix times matrix multiplication. For reasons that will be discussed in section 5.4, the higher BLAS-level routines run faster than the lower level ones. As shown in Table 3.1, optimized level-3 BLAS frequently come close to the peak speed of the machine. By reordering loops in a code it is frequently possible to replace several calls to lower level BLAS by a single call to a higher level routine. This was done in the program blaslevel.f, listed in section A.1 of the appendix, which was used to obtain the timing results in Table 3.1 for three BLAS routines representative of each level. Even though the vendor-supplied BLAS routines are usually well optimized, exceptions exist, particularly on new computer models. If the time spent in BLAS routines is significant, it is a good practice to verify by timing (as will be explained in Chapter 4) whether the performance of BLAS is reasonable. If the loops are very short, the overhead of calling a BLAS routine can become prohibitive. Even a moderately optimized user-written loop structure can be faster in this case. Cray compilers automatically replace user-written loop structures by matching level-2 and level-3 BLAS routines, unless the loops are expected to be short.

A very good quality public domain library is LAPACK, containing all the standard dense linear algebra operations, such as the solution of linear systems of equations, singular value decompositions and eigenvalue problems. It supersedes the older LINPACK and EISPACK libraries. This library is built on top of the BLAS library, leading to very good performance, particularly if a vendor-optimized version of BLAS is utilized. Some of the LAPACK routines can also be found in optimized form in some of the vendors' mathematical libraries. Further information on LA-PACK can be found in its users' guide [7] or at http://www.netlib.org/index.html.

In addition to these public domain libraries, several computer manufacturers provide scientific libraries containing additional routines, such as special functions, fast Fourier transforms, integration and curve fitting routines. The ESSL library from IBM and the LIBSCI library from Cray contain very efficient algorithmic implementations for their specific architecture.

There are other libraries available (http://gams.nist.gov), both commercially (such as the NAG or IMSL library) or in the public domain (in the NETLIB repository http://www.netlib.org/ for example), but the efficiency and numerical quality of these routines vary widely.

Exercise: Find the location of the BLAS library on your computer (typically either in /lib, /usr/lib, or /usr/local/lib) and measure the speed of three routines belonging to different BLAS levels.

3.3 Optimal data layout

This very important aspect of any optimization work, the layout of all the data structures needed in the calculation, should take place before the writing of the program starts. Data that are processed in sequence should be located close to each other in the physical memory. This will ensure "data locality," meaning that data that are brought in cache will be used at least once before being flushed out of cache. Thus, the high cost of a cache miss is distributed among several memory accesses.

For instance, a Fortran77 array containing the positions of a collection of n particles should be dimensioned as

```
dimension r(3,n)
```

instead of

```
dimension r(n,3)
```

since most likely the three spatial coordinates for a given particle will be accessed consecutively. The same considerations apply to data structures defined in Fortran90. Sometimes, different data structures could be optimal in different parts of a program. In this case, it is important to carefully weigh the relative importance of these two sections of the code to decide which data structure will give better overall efficiency. These considerations should be taken very seriously. Low performance due to a poor data layout embedded in the structure of a program may not be possible to be improved by the application of the optimization techniques meant to improve data locality.

3.4   Use of compiler optimizations

Programs compiled without any optimization usually run very slowly on RISC architectures. Using a medium optimization level ($-O2$ on many machines) typically leads to a speedup by factors of 2 to 3 without a significant increase in compilation time. Using the highest available optimization levels can lead to further performance improvements, but to performance deterioration as well. The compiler applies transformation rules, based on heuristics, that in most cases improve performance. Since the compiler does not have all the necessary information to determine whether certain transformations of the program will pay off, the success of the transformations is not guaranteed. It is certainly worthwhile to try several optimization levels and possibly some other compiler options as well, and to assess their effect on the overall program speed. For example, compiler options that generate code targeted at a specific processor architecture are generally useful: $-$qarch on IBM, $-$arch on Compaq and $-$TARG on SGI.

Similar considerations apply to preprocessors. The rule of thumb for compiler preprocessors is that they can help to improve performance of poorly written programs. In a reasonably well written program, most of the transformations generated by preprocessors apply to the unoptimized portions of the code, those portions that take little of the total runtime. These transformations have no other effect than unnecessarily increasing the size of the executable. In well-written hotspots of a code, preprocessors generally fail to further improve the performance. Overall, chances are that preprocessors will slow down the program rather than speeding it up. One good practice allowing preprocessors and compilers to discriminately apply optimal transformations is the use of compiler directives. Compiler directives indicate the type of transformations expected and the precise portion of a code where they need to be applied. Unfortunately, compiler directives are not standardized across platforms resulting in a loss of portability.

3.5   Basic optimizations done by the compiler

Modern compilers are capable of performing a large variety of optimizations [5, 8, 9]. In order to avoid time-consuming manual optimizations it is important to know what kind of transformation can be effectively performed by compilers.

Compilers do optimizations on units called basic blocks. A basic block is a segment of code that does not contain branches. Consequently, all the instructions in a basic block will always be executed together. A basic block too big to be processed can be subdivided into overlapping units called windows. The compiler repeatedly walks through these windows, performing optimizations within each window. In this section we will briefly present different types of standard optimizations done by modern compilers.

- Common subexpression elimination: If a subexpression is common to two or more expressions, the compiler will pull it out and precalculate it. In the example below, the compiler will detect that $(a + b)$ is common to the expression for both $s1$ and $s2$.

```
s1 = a + b + c
s2 = a + b - c
```

Thus it is not necessary to introduce a temporary variable for the common subexpression, as shown below. The compiler will do exactly this and reduce the number of additions/subtractions from four to three.

```
t = a + b
s1 = t + c
s2 = t - c
```

However, there are some pitfalls to this technique. Let us consider the following code segment where the order of the additions/subtractions is changed.

```
s1 = a + c + b
s2 = a + b - c
```

In Fortran, statements are read from left to right. This means that the statement $a + b + c$ is identical to $(a + b) + c$, whereas $a + c + b$ is identical to $(a + c) + b$. Because commutivativity does not hold for floating point operations these two expressions are not bitwise identical. According to the Fortran standard [1], the compiler is allowed to do a transformation between the two forms. However, not all compilers will do it, or perhaps will do it only at the highest optimization level. To help the compiler to spot common subexpressions, it is good practice to put them in parentheses:

```
s1 = (a + b) + c
s2 = (a + b) - c
```

Using parentheses is also the only way to enforce a certain order of evaluation in case this is necessary for numerical stability.

Another, less obvious common subexpression is encountered when referring to the same array element in different lines of the code. The common subexpression here is the load of the array element. In the following segment of code:

```
r = 2.*x(i)
s = x(i)-1.
```

the optimizing compiler will produce an instruction schedule corresponding to

```
t1=x(i)
r = 2.*t1
s = t1-1.
```

Compilers will not eliminate subexpressions involving user-defined functions. The reason for this is that parameters could be changed in a way that is invisible to the calling routine, for example, through the use of common blocks. This could lead to different results even if the visible arguments are the same. An easy example is the random number function. Obviously the code segment

```
x=rand() + rand()**2
```

is not the same as

```
tt=rand()
x=tt + tt**2
```

In Fortran95 a user-defined function can be declared "pure," meaning that it has no side effects of the kind described before. In this case the compiler can eliminate subexpressions.

- Strength reduction: Strength reduction is the replacement of an arithmetic expression by another equivalent expression which can be evaluated faster. A typical example is the replacement of $2*i$ by $i + i$, since integer additions are usually faster than integer multiplications. This particular example would lead to no improvements for floating point numbers since floating point additions and multiplications take the same number of cycles on a modern processor. A typical strength reduction for floating point numbers is the replacement of $x**2$ by $x*x$. As will be discussed in more detail in the context of special functions, exponentiation typically takes a few hundred cycles. Because of precision requirements, the compiler is rather conservative about strength reductions. For instance, IBM's XLF compiler (version 4.01) will replace $x**3$ by $x*x*x$, but not higher powers, even though this would be more efficient. If several powers of x, say x, $x**2$, $x**3$ and $x**4$, are needed in the program, this particular compiler will recursively generate them by multiplications. Idiosyncrasies of the compiler are present here too. Let's assume that a section of the program requires the calculations of $x**11$, $x**12$, $x**13$ and $x**14$. Most compilers will probably call the exponentiation routine four times instead of recursively generating the higher powers of x from $x**11$.

- Loop-invariant code motion: Let us assume the following loop in a program:

```
do 10,i=1,n
   a(i)=r*s*a(i)
enddo
```

The compiler will precalculate $r*s$ outside the loop, with the same effect as in the following hand-tuned version:

```
t1=r*s
do i=1,n
    a(i)=t1*a(i)
enddo
```

Because commutativity transformations are not always applied, the compiler will frequently not carry out this transformation if the loop is written as

```
do i=1,n
    a(i)=r*a(i)*s
enddo
```

As in the case of the common subexpression elimination, it is therefore good practice to bracket the loop-invariant quantities.

- Constant value propagation and evaluation: Whenever the compiler can determine that a variable takes on a constant value, it will replace all the occurrences of this variable by this constant value. Also, when an expression involves several constant values, they will be calculated and replaced by a new constant value. These two processes are illustrated in the following example:

```
two=2.d0
x=3.d0*two*y
```

After optimization the example above is equivalent to

```
x=6.d0*y
```

- Induction variable simplification: This technique applies mainly to the calculation of array addresses. Induction variables are variables whose value is a linear function of the loop counter. Let us consider the following code segment

```
dimension a(4,100)
do i=1,100
    x=x+a(1,i)
enddo
```

The relative address of $a(1,i)$, with respect to the first array element $a(1,1)$, is $4*i - 4$. Calculating the address in this way would require expensive integer multiplications. The optimized code generated by the compiler corresponds to the Fortran code:

```
dimension a(4*100)
iadd=1
do i=1,100
    x=x+a(iadd)
    iadd=iadd+4
enddo
```

where the relative address iadd is now calculated recursively by fast additions.

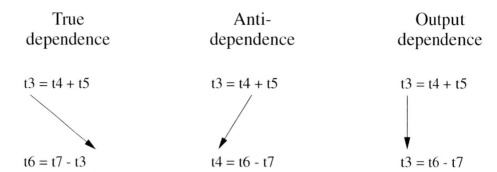

True dependence	Anti- dependence	Output dependence
t3 = t4 + t5	t3 = t4 + t5	t3 = t4 + t5
t6 = t7 - t3	t4 = t6 - t7	t3 = t6 - t7

Figure 3.1: *The standard classification of dependencies. The scalar variables t3, t4, etc. are assumed to correspond to registers.*

- Register allocation and instruction scheduling: This part of the optimization phase is by far the most difficult, but also the most important one. There are no deterministic non–NP-complete algorithms that would allow these problems to be solved in an optimal way in all cases. Practical implementations are largely based on heuristics and can therefore lead to nonoptimal results. A detailed description of the problems involved here is clearly beyond the scope of this book. We will only summarize a few basic principles. The main goal of this optimization phase is to eliminate dependencies. The standard types of dependencies are illustrated in Figure 3.1. Two dependent instructions cannot be executed simultaneously, nor in consecutive cycles. The second dependent instruction has to wait, usually a few cycles, before the first one is finished. The compiler attempts to order dependent instructions in such a way that they are separated by a few cycles or, if possible, to eliminate them. Let us look at a few examples.

```
x=1.+2.*y
s=s+x
z=2.+3.*r
t=t+z
```

In this first example we note two true dependencies. The second and fourth instruction need the result from the first and third instruction. On several RISC processors, the statements in lines 1 and 3 correspond to a single instruction, the fused multiply-add (FMA) (see section 5.1). Specifically, on an IBM Power architecture, a new instruction of this type can start in each cycle, but the result is available after two cycles only. With the ordering shown above, there would be one idle cycle after the first and third instruction. This idle cycle can easily be eliminated by reordering the instructions as shown below:

```
x=1.+2.*y
z=2.+3.*r
s=s+x
t=t+z
```

During the first cycle, the first FMA starts. During the second cycle, the second FMA is originated, while the first FMA finishes. In the third and fourth cycles, respectively, the first and second additions are executed. Altogether, the computation takes four cycles only, compared to six cycles in the original version. An optimizing compiler will rearrange the instructions in this more efficient way.

Let us now look at the antidependency and output dependency in Figure 3.1. These dependencies can be eliminated by renaming the registers. In the case of an antidependency, we can write the second result in register t2 instead of t4. In the case of the output dependency, we can use register t2 for one of the two results instead of using t3 for both.

As a consequence of these optimizations, the sequence of instructions in the compiler-generated code will be different from the one in the original program. Even instructions that are on the same line in a Fortran code can be far apart in the assembler output. In particular, an attempt is made to move loads ahead in order to eliminate delays from load latencies. As was briefly mentioned in the chapter on computer architecture, loads can take a large number of cycles if they cause a cache miss. This delay can be hidden if the load is far ahead of the instruction using the loaded item. The only constraint is that the instruction remains within the same basic block.

The allocation of registers cannot be completely controlled. The register allocation is based on a representation of the code in terms of graphs, where name definitions for scalar variables and array elements are completely lost. In most cases, this is probably beneficial, as illustrated by the antidependence and output dependence columns in Figure 3.1, which could easily be removed by a better register allocation. In advanced optimization work, it would be desirable to have an influence on register allocation. This is currently not possible with any of the commercially available compilers.

Chapter 4

Timing and Profiling of a Program

The starting point of any optimization work is the timing and profiling of the program. Timing and profiling are the means to determine the performance of a code. The measured time, together with either estimates or counts of the number of floating point operations, allows us to calculate the speed, usually measured in Mflops (millions of floating point operations per second). With hardware performance monitors (discussed in section 4.5), the speed is directly available.

A comparison between the measured Mflops and the peak Mflops rates for that machine gives a good indication of the efficiency of your program. The dividing line between acceptable and poor performance is, of course, disputable. One rule of thumb is that for large-scale scientific applications 50% of peak performance is very good, albeit hard to achieve, whereas less than 10% should be an indication that optimization work is in order. In this order of magnitude type of analysis, contrasting the performance of your code with existing benchmarks for similar computations can be helpful, too, as explained in Chapter 10.

For the interpretation of the output of the timing and profiling tools it is necessary to understand the various time metrics that are used.

The most important time measure is the CPU time. This is the time in which the CPU is dedicated to the execution of a program. It is the sum of two parts, the user time and the system time. The user time is the time spent executing the instructions of the program. The system time is the time spent by the operating system for service operations requested by the program. In general, the system component of the CPU time is small compared to the user component of the CPU time. If it is not, this is an indication of an inefficiency in the code.

Another important metric is the elapsed or wallclock time. If several programs are running on a computer, the total execution time of one program will be longer than its CPU time. Assuming that three programs are running with the same priority, the elapsed time will be roughly three times the CPU time. Even in standalone (i.e., when a single code is running on the computer), the CPU will timeshare between that code and pure systems tasks. Because of this, the elapsed time will be longer than the CPU time.

Some service operations cannot be traced back uniquely to the execution of a certain program. Paging is a well-known example in this context. If two programs with large memory requirements are running concurrently, the total amount of paging is much larger than if they are running one after the other. Paging time is therefore not counted as CPU time, but as elapsed time. In the same way, cache and TLB misses can partially increment the elapsed time instead of the CPU time. If, in standalone, the elapsed time is much larger than the user time, this is an indication of an inefficient program.

Overall timing information of a program can be obtained using the UNIX commands "timex" or "time." This simply involves preceding the running command for the code, say "a.out," by the "timex" or "time" command, such as "time a.out." At the end of the run, the CPU time, split up in user and system time, and the elapsed time will be printed out. The exact format of this timing output varies among different vendors, but is described in the "man" pages.

Because of the ambiguities and interference effects mentioned above, there are always considerable fluctuations in measured times. Even in standalone, fluctuations of a few percentage points are normal. When the machine is shared with other jobs, these fluctuations can be even bigger.

The first thing to know when starting to optimize a program is which parts of it take most of the runtime, i.e., the identification of the "hotspots." Profiling the program will answer this question. Several profiling techniques are available and will be discussed in the next sections.

4.1   Subroutine-level profiling

A subroutine-level profile is obtained by compiling the program with a special compiler flag, usually "−p." The compiler will then insert timing calls at the beginning and end of each subroutine. At execution time, the timing information is written to a file, typically "mon.out." The "prof" command allows you to read in the information contained in this file and to analyze the code in the form of a "profile." Let us profile the following short program:

```
      implicit real*8 (a-h,o-z)
      parameter(nexp=13,n=2**nexp)
      dimension x(n)
      do 15,i=1,n
15    x(i)=1.234d0
      do ic=1,1000
        call sub1(n,x,sum1)
        call sub2(n,x,sum2)
      enddo
      write(6,*) sum1,sum2
      end
```

```
      subroutine sub1(n,x,sum)
      implicit real*8 (a-h,o-z)
      dimension x(n)
      sum=0.d0
      do 10,i=1,n
10    sum=sum+2.d0*x(i)+(x(i)-1.d0)**2+3.d0+i*1.d-20-4.d0*(i-200)**2
      return
      end

      subroutine sub2(n,x,sum)
      implicit real*8 (a-h,o-z)
      dimension x(n)
      sum=0.d0
      do 10,i=1,n
10    sum=sum+x(i)**.3333333333d0
      return
      end
```

On an IBM Power2, the output obtained from the "prof" command looks like this:

Name	%Time	Seconds	Cumsecs	#Calls	msec/call
._pow	63.8	21.11	21.11	8192000	0.0026
.__mcount	28.4	9.39	30.50		
.sub1	3.8	1.27	31.77	1000	1.270
.sub2	2.3	0.77	32.54	1000	0.770
.					
.					

First, it is apparent that the time spent in the compiler library functions is not attributed to the subroutines from which they are called, but to the functions themselves (the exponentiation function is called from subroutine sub2). As a result, if the same library function is called from several subroutines, it is not possible to find out directly which subroutine invokes them more frequently and thus takes more time. Second, we note an additional category "mcount," which is the time spent in the timing routines themselves, i.e., the overhead of profiling. This can be a significant fraction of the total execution time and it can bias the timing analysis. Calls to subroutines that are part of libraries, such as BLAS, cannot be analyzed in this way.

4.2 Tick-based profiling

All these drawbacks can be avoided by using profiling utilities based on tick counting statistics. Each time the operating system interrupts the execution of a program (usually every 1/100th of a second), such a profiling tool will identify in which subroutine the interrupt occurred and augment the number of ticks associated with that subroutine. If the program is compiled with additional options (usually "-g"), such tools can even trace back the interrupt to the line number of your program and profile at code line level. Unfortunately, such profiling tools frequently fail to assign the correct line of code to the instruction, assigning it instead to neighboring lines. With IBM's xlf compiler, the exact sequence of commands to use is the following:

```
xlf -g myprog.f
tprof a.out
```

For the subroutine in the program above the line level profiling output looks as follows:

```
Ticks Profile for sub6 in prof.f


  Line   Ticks   Source

   72      -          sum=0.d0
   73      -          do 10,i=1,n
   74     913    10   sum=sum+x(i)**.3333333333d0
   75      -          return
   76      -          end

913 Total Ticks for sub6 in prof.f
```

4.3   Timing small sections of your program

Very often we need to know the CPU time spent in a code's hotspots. By calculating the number of floating point operations executed in hotspots, the timing information allows the calculation of the sustained speed. This is done by manually inserting timing calls.

```
real t1,t2
integer count1,count2,count_rate,countmax


call system_clock(count1,count_rate,count_max)
call cpu_time(t1)

.. code to be timed ...

call cpu_time(t2)
call system_clock(count2,count_rate,count_max)

print*, 'CPU time (sec)',t2-t1
print*, 'elapsed time (sec)',(count2-count1)/float(count_rate)
```

The Fortran90 standard provides for two functions that measure the CPU time and the elapsed time, as shown above. As in the case of profiling, the time spent in these timing routines, i.e., the overhead of timing, can be significant if they are called very frequently.

In Fortran77 the situation is quite confusing, since each vendor has different timing routines. Table 4.1 gives the names and attributes of CPU timers on a variety of machines that can be used for Fortran77 or Fortran90 codes in those cases where the Fortran90 timing functions are not yet implemented.

The elapsed time can be measured from within a Fortran77 program on Cray, Compaq, IBM and SGI by using the function "timef()."

Table 4.1: *CPU timing routines that can be called from Fortran programs on different computers. It is assumed that the variable "cpu" is double precision.*

```
| COMPUTER          |      ATTRIBUTE      |       SYNTAX           |
| ----------------------------------------------------------------
|----------------------------------------------------------------
| CRAY vector       | real SECOND         | cpu=SECOND()           |
|----------------------------------------------------------------
| CRAY T3E          | real TSECND         | cpu=TSECND()           |
|----------------------------------------------------------------
| Compaq/DEC Alpha  | real*4 ETIME,tarray(2) | cpu=dble(ETIME(tarray)) |
| HP                |                     |                        |
| SUN               |                     |                        |
|----------------------------------------------------------------
| FUJITSU           |                     | call CLOCK(cpu,1,2)    |
|                   |                     | cpu=cpu*1.d-3          |
|----------------------------------------------------------------
| HITACHI           |                     | call XCLOCK(cpu,8)     |
|----------------------------------------------------------------
| IBM RS6000        | integer MCLOCK      | cpu=dble(MCLOCK())*1.d-2 |
|----------------------------------------------------------------|
| SGI               |                     |                        |
|----------------------------------------------------------------
| NEC               |                     | call CLOCK(cpu)        |
|----------------------------------------------------------------
```

A Fortran90 package containing easy-to-use timing functions with enhanced functionality can be obtained from: http://math.nist.gov/mcsd/Staff/WMitchell/stopwatch/. At the time of this writing, this package was enabled on the Cray vector machines, as well as on Compaq, IBM, HP and SUN workstations.

A possible problem with this analysis method is that the resolution of the timing routines is usually fairly coarse (1/100 of a second for "mclock," 1/1000 for most others). In order to get good statistics, the runtime of the hotspot has to be much longer than this resolution. Frequently this necessitates artificially repeating the execution of the hotspot by bracketing it with an additional timing loop. Since in these repeated executions data can be available in cache at the beginning of a new timing iteration, the performance numbers can be artificially high. In order to avoid this pitfall, a call to a cache flushing routine has to be inserted at the beginning of each timing iteration. Any routine that refreshes all the cache lines can be used as a cache flushing routine.

Exercise: Write a fast cache flushing routine. Should it be based on loads or on stores? What is the optimal stride?

In timing runs one has to make sure that no floating point exceptions (such as overflows) are present, since they will increase the CPU time. Testing with zeros can also be problematic on some machines. Some compilers are able to figure out that the numerical results of the timing loops are never utilized and do not execute those loops at all. In this way, the speed of the program can get close to infinity! Therefore, it is a good practice to print out some of the numerical results of a timing run in order to make sure that the compiler is not outsmarting you.

4.4   Assembler output

Compilers generate an assembler language version of a program, containing a translation of Fortran or C code into elementary instructions. The size and form of the instruction set is different for computers from different vendors. The RISC machines we are concentrating on typically have a smaller number of elementary instructions compared to older complex instruction set computers (CISC), though this difference tends to be less stringent lately. Typical instructions are loads and stores, which load and store numerical values from cache/memory into the registers, and additions and multiplications for integers and floating point variables. Best performance could be achieved by programming directly in assembler language. This would not only be very time consuming and error prone but also lead to nonportable code. This is no longer an alternative.

However, for in-depth optimization work it is very useful to look at the assembler language output generated by the compiler. This reveals the instructions that the computer will eventually execute and the sequence in which it will do so. On IBM machines, an easily readable pseudoassembler output is generated by using the compiler flags "−qlist −qsource." An important piece of information included is the estimated number of cycles for each instruction. On the SGI machines, a similar pseudoassembler listing is generated using the options "−Flist=on, −PHASE:flist=on." On many other machines, the assembler language output can be obtained by using the compiler option "−S." An inspection of assembler output will show that, in general, the compiler is not doing a perfect job in optimizing the code, even when invoked at the highest optimization level available (typically "−O3" to "−O5"). The assembler listing could be used to check the effect of code restructuring on the mixture of instructions that the compiler generates. In many cases compilers undo hand-optimized code restructuring. It is frequently possible to obtain performance improvements by making changes in the assembler output and to execute the program with the modified assembler code.

4.5   Hardware performance monitors

Several vendors provide hardware performance monitors that give very detailed information about the execution history of a program, such as the number of floating point instructions, the number of cycles, the number of memory accesses and the number of cache misses. This information can be highly useful for optimization work. A number of caveats, though, are in order. The output is frequently ambiguous and the user interface is sometimes clumsy. Hardware performance monitors can give different results for measured parameters that one would expect to be constant across machines for identical programs, such as the total number of floating point operations. This can be due to the evaluation of special functions, such as exponentials, that internally requires floating point operations. Such floating point operations can be added to the other, nonhidden, floating point operations or be counted separately. Moreover, different algorithms exist for the evaluation of these special functions that differ in the number of floating point operations. Different vendors are likely to use different algorithms. Some arithmetic operations, such as divisions, are performed by special hardware on some machines. Even when a program contains straightforward floating point additions and multiplications, ambiguities could still be present. The statement

```
s = t*x + t*y
```

could be changed by the compiler to

```
s = t*(x + y)
```

thus reducing the number of floating point operations. The output from SGI's hardware performance monitor invoked by "perfex a.out" for two loops that will be discussed in detail in section 6.3 is shown below for out of cache data sizes. A memory access problem surfaces, since the number of caches misses is equal to the number of loads/stores.

```
first output: -O2, good loop order.


 0 Cycles.....................................................  2510908272
 1 Issued instructions........................................  3623280800
 2 Issued loads...............................................   102465536
 3 Issued stores..............................................   101166064
 4 Issued store conditionals..................................           0
 5 Failed store conditionals..................................           0
 6 Decoded branches...........................................   102210624
 7 Quadwords written back from scache.........................    23840624
 8 Correctable scache data array ECC errors...................           0
 9 Primary instruction cache misses...........................       57152
10 Secondary instruction cache misses.........................          16
11 Instruction misprediction from scache way prediction table..        4352
12 External interventions.....................................        1120
13 External invalidations.....................................       52864
14 Virtual coherency conditions...............................           0
15 Graduated instructions.....................................  3535675424
16 Cycles.....................................................  2510908272
17 Graduated instructions.....................................  3609837104
18 Graduated loads............................................   100845632
19 Graduated stores...........................................   100096736
20 Graduated store conditionals...............................           0
21 Graduated floating point instructions......................           0
22 Quadwords written back from primary data cache.............    24835488
23 TLB misses.................................................       26464
24 Mispredicted branches......................................      101296
25 Primary data cache misses..................................    24741216 <---
26 Secondary data cache misses................................     6156784
27 Data misprediction from scache way prediction table.........        2400
28 External intervention hits in scache.......................         544
29 External invalidation hits in scache.......................       29408
30 Store/prefetch exclusive to clean block in scache..........        1504

second output: -O2 bad loop order


 0 Cycles.....................................................  5068958784
 1 Issued instructions........................................  4001498064
```

```
 2 Issued loads............................................   102565536
 3 Issued stores...........................................   101866064
 4 Issued store conditionals...............................           0
 5 Failed store conditionals...............................           0
 6 Decoded branches........................................   126295552
 7 Quadwords written back from scache......................    25093600
 8 Correctable scache data array ECC errors................           0
 9 Primary instruction cache misses........................      152352
10 Secondary instruction cache misses......................        9184
11 Instruction misprediction from scache way prediction table..   45760
12 External interventions..................................         992
13 External invalidations..................................      105584
14 Virtual coherency conditions............................           0
15 Graduated instructions..................................  3547257504
16 Cycles..................................................  5068958784
17 Graduated instructions..................................  3543313280
18 Graduated loads.........................................    97208640
19 Graduated stores........................................    99135552
20 Graduated store conditionals............................           0
21 Graduated floating point instructions...................           0
22 Quadwords written back from primary data cache..........   184194352
23 TLB misses..............................................    25569840
24 Mispredicted branches...................................      105040
25 Primary data cache misses...............................   198816688 <---
26 Secondary data cache misses.............................     7099472
27 Data misprediction from scache way prediction table.....    25549328
28 External intervention hits in scache....................          32
29 External invalidation hits in scache....................       61184
30 Store/prefetch exclusive to clean block in scache.......        4224
```

Another source of ambiguity that can be found on SGI machines is related to the counting of fused multiply-adds (SGI's "madd" instruction). The SGI hardware performance monitor, invoked by the "perfex" command, shows the number of floating point instructions by counting a fused multiply-add as a single instruction, not as two instructions, as would be required for the calculation of the sustained speed in Mflops. To overcome this difficulty, two runs of the program with perfex are needed. In the first run, the program should be compiled with all needed compiler options plus $-$TARG:madd $=$ off, which prevents the compiler from using fused multiply-add instruction in the assembler code. From this first run, the total number of floating point operations is obtained from the reading of event 21 from the hardware performance monitor's output. The second needed run requires the recompilation of the program without this compiler flag. This run should be timed, or the runtime inferred from event 0 (total number of cycles). The correct sustained speed is then calculated by dividing the number of floating point operations from the first run by the time obtained in the second run.

A very useful analysis tool that combines tick-based profiling with the output from the hardware performance monitor is the Digital/Compaq continuous profiling tool (http://www.research.digital.com/SRC/dcpi/).

4.6   Profiling parallel programs

Fairly sophisticated parallel performance analysis tools are available from several vendors. Their drawback is that they are not easy to use, have limited capabilities (for instance, they work interactively but not in batch) and are intrusive (thus considerably modifying the timing profile of the code). The learning curve for being able to use such tools efficiently is quite significant too.

It is customary to use the elapsed time as the metric for parallel code execution. One of the reasons for this is that the assignment of the communication time to either CPU or system time is ambiguous. When not running in standalone, contention for communication resources will be present, making it difficult to decide whether the communication took a certain amount of time by itself or was slowed down by the interference with other programs. In addition, waiting times at barriers, which may be the result of load imbalance, are usually not included in the CPU time.

The timing routine "timing," listed in section A.2 of the appendix, can be utilized for timing serial and parallel programs. Below we present a sample program instrumented for timing with the "timing" subroutine.

```
        program time_mpi
c sums the rows and columns of a square matrix in parallel
        implicit real*8 (a-h,o-z)
        logical parallel
        include 'mpif.h'
c serial or parallel
        parameter(parallel=.true.)
c repeat to get long enough measuring interval
        parameter(nrep=100000,nrec=100)
c dimension of matrix
        parameter(nprc=4)
        dimension aa(nprc),bb(nprc)

        if (parallel) then
c if parallel initialize MPI
        write(6,*) 'start mpi'
        call MPI_INIT(ierr)
        call MPI_COMM_RANK(MPI_COMM_WORLD,iproc,ierr)
        call MPI_COMM_SIZE(MPI_COMM_WORLD,nproc,ierr)
        write(6,*) 'mpi started',iproc,nproc
        if (iproc.eq.0) write(6,*) 'nproc=',nproc
        if (nproc.ne.nprc) stop 'wrong number of processors'
        else
c if run serially
        iproc=0
        nproc=1
        endif
c initialize timing routine
        call timing(' ','INI',0,iproc,nproc)
c each processor initializes its column (aa(i,j)=i)
        do 10,i=1,nproc
10      aa(i)=i
c each processors sums column
        nflop=nproc*nrep
        call timing('SUMS ','STR',nflop,iproc,nproc)
        do irep=1,nrep
          sum=0.d0
          do i=1,nproc
            sum=sum+aa(i)
          enddo
        enddo
```

```
        call timing('SUMS ','END',nflop,iproc,nproc)
        write(6,*) 'processor, sum',iproc,sum
c transpose matrix
        nflop=nproc*nrec
        call timing('TRANSP','STR',nflop,iproc,nproc)
        if (parallel) then
          do irep=1,nrec
            call MPI_ALLTOALL(aa,1,MPI_DOUBLE_PRECISION,
1                             bb,1,MPI_DOUBLE_PRECISION,
1                             MPI_COMM_WORLD,ierr)
          enddo
        else
          bb(1)=aa(1)
        endif
        call timing('TRANSP','END',nflop,iproc,nproc)
c each processors sums column of transposed matrix (row of original matrix)
        nflop=nproc*nrep
        call timing('SUMS ','STR',nflop,iproc,nproc)
        do irep=1,nrep
          sum=0.d0
          do i=1,nproc
            sum=sum+bb(i)
          enddo
        enddo
        call timing('SUMS ','END',nflop,iproc,nproc)
        write(6,*) 'processor, T sum',iproc,sum
c finalize timing routine
        call timing(' ','FIN',0,iproc,nproc)
        if (parallel) then
          call MPI_FINALIZE(ierr)
        endif
        end
```

The output of this run on a four-processor IBM SP2 is shown below. Since each processor did exactly the same amount of work, the deviation in the number of Flops is zero. However, we note a small deviation in the execution time on different processors. If a communication step (MPI_ALLTOALL) is analyzed with this tool, then "nflop" is the amount of data to be sent or received. The output file will then print in this category the number of Msends/Mreceives per second, instead of Mflops. The fact that the total execution time ("total") equals in this example the sum of all timing categories ("sum") means that we have included all relevant parts of the program in the timing procedure by defining the appropriate timing categories, and that the overhead of the timing calls was negligible.

```
CATEGORY , TIME(sec) + dev , PERCENT ,   FLOPS + dev ,    SPEED(Mflp)
SUMS        .450E-01 .50E-02  42.857    .800E+06 .00E+00   .178E+02
TRANSP      .600E-01 .23E-01  57.143    .400E+03 .00E+00   .667E-02
SUM         .105E+00
TOTAL       .105E+00
4  processors
```

Chapter 5

Optimization of Floating Point Operations

As we have pointed out several times, memory access problems are usually the single most detrimental factor leading to large performance degradation. Nevertheless, we will start our optimization discussion with the topic of floating point operations. As a matter of fact, when tuning a program, it is recommended to start by addressing this type of optimization before moving on to memory access optimizations. In order to discern the effect of floating point optimizations, it is necessary to eliminate limiting effects due to memory access issues. In the floating point optimization phase this can be easily achieved by working with small data sets that fit in cache, even though they may not represent the memory requirements of a realistic application. Consequently, we will assume in this section that all the necessary data are available in cache and that therefore cache misses do not limit performance. The topic of memory access optimization will be taken up in detail in the next chapter.

In general, floating point operations dominate in "number-crunching" scientific codes. This is in contrast to other applications, such as compilers or editors, that are integer-arithmetic bound. We will not analyze integer performance in detail in this book. Even though the "useful" operations in most of the scientific codes are floating point operations, integer operations occur frequently too. For example, they are needed to calculate the addresses of array elements, with the effect that practically all load or store operations require integer arithmetic. As a matter of fact, the load and store operations on several architectures are handled by the integer unit. In this book we will not distinguish between the calculation of the address and the process of transferring data from the cache into the registers, but instead consider loads and stores each as style operations.

5.1   Fused multiply-add instructions

The fused multiply-add instruction (FMA), found on several modern architectures (see Table 2.1), provides for the execution of a multiplication followed by an addition $(a + b*c)$ as a single instruction. This reduces the latency compared to the case where a separate multiplication and addition is used and makes the instruction scheduling easier for the compiler. Because commutativity transformations (see section 3.5) are not always applied, care has to be taken to write the code in such a way that the compiler can identify this instruction. For instance, if the following line of code

```
a=b+c*d+f*g
```

is written as

```
a=f*g+c*d+b
```

two separate multiplies and additions are needed, resulting in roughly doubled execution time. Very aggressive compiler optimization levels will generally do the commutativity transformation, generating an instruction sequence of two FMA instructions. For optimality in this line of code, it is still necessary to eliminate the dependency of the two FMA instructions. The technique for eliminating dependencies will be explained in the next section.

5.2   Exposing instruction-level parallelism in a program

As mentioned in section 2.1, superscalar CPUs have a high degree of on-chip parallelism. The same degree of parallelism has to be exposed in the program in order to achieve the best efficiency. As an illustration, let us look at a simple vector norm calculation.

```
      program length
      parameter(n=2**14)
      dimension a(n)
      subroutine lngth1(n,a,tt)
      implicit real*8 (a-h,o-z)
      dimension a(n)
      tt=0.d0
      do 100,j=1,n
        tt=tt+a(j)*a(j)
100   continue
      return
      end
```

We aim to optimize this vector norm subroutine on an IBM 590 workstation. From Table 2.1 we see that this processor has two floating point units. However, the program has only one independent stream and thus cannot keep two units busy. Furthermore, we see that the output tt of one FMA is the input for the next FMA.

Hence, we have a dependency. Since the latency of the FMA is two cycles, we cannot start a new FMA every cycle, as it would be possible if we had independent operations. With this in mind we restructure the program as follows.

```
      subroutine lngth4(n,a,tt)
c works correctly only if the array size is a multiple of 4
      implicit real*8 (a-h,o-z)
      dimension a(n)
      t1=0.d0
      t2=0.d0
      t3=0.d0
      t4=0.d0
      do 100,j=1,n-3,4
c first floating point unit, all even cycles
         t1=t1+a(j+0)*a(j+0)
c first floating point unit, all odd cycles
         t2=t2+a(j+1)*a(j+1)
c second floating point unit, all even cycles
         t3=t3+a(j+2)*a(j+2)
c second floating point unit, all odd cycles
         t4=t4+a(j+3)*a(j+3)
100      continue
      tt=t1+t2+t3+t4
      return
      end
```

Exercise: Generalize the subroutine lngth4 in such a way that it gives the correct result for data sets of arbitrary length.

This kind of transformation is called loop unrolling. Its effect is that it usually improves the availability of parallelism within a loop. The number of independent streams generated by loop unrolling—four in the subroutine lngth4—is called the depth of the unrolling. On an IBM 590 workstation, the unrolled version runs at peak speed (260 Mflops), whereas the original version runs at just one-fourth of the peak speed. Of course, this is true only for data sets that are cache resident.

Most compilers will try to do optimizations of this type when invoked with the highest optimization level. Even in this simple example some subtleties are present. Straightforward, compiler-generated loop unrolling will not lead to the same code as our hand-optimized code, but to the following code instead:

```
      subroutine lngth4a(n,a,tt)
c works correctly only if the array size is multiple of 4
      implicit real*8 (a-h,o-z)
      dimension a(n)
      tt=0.d0
      do 100,j=1,n-3,4
        tt=tt+a(j+0)*a(j+0)+a(j+1)*a(j+1)+a(j+2)*a(j+2)+a(j+3)*a(j+3)
100 continue
      return
      end
```

This unrolled code will give a bitwise identical result to the original one. Splitting up this single stream into four independent ones does not lead to bitwise identical results. As an aside, it turns out that the numerical accuracy obtained by summing with several streams is usually higher than when using a single stream. If the

IBM XLF Fortran compiler (version 4.01) is invoked with the "−O3 −qarch=pwr2 −qtune=pwr2" flags, it produces an assembler output corresponding exactly to the hand-optimized version, therefore running at peak speed. An older version of the compiler (3.02) does the unrolling shown in lngth4a, without introducing four independent streams necessary to eliminate the dependencies, no matter which compiler flags are utilized. On the SGI Origin 2000, the Fortran compiler (MIPSpro_7.2.1), with the optimization flags "−O3 −mips4," provides for two independent data streams, which should be enough for this architecture. This leads to a speed of 350 Mflops, close to the machine's 390 Mflops peak. The hand-optimized version lngth4, with four independent data streams, runs slightly faster, namely at 375 Mflops. On the Compaq EV6 (500 Mhz) workstation the compiler (version V5.2) was not able to create independent streams and the attained speed was only 250 Mflops out of a peak of 1000 Mflops. Unrolling the loop by hand to a depth of 8 and compiling it with options that prevent the compiler from doing loop transformations (f77 −O2 −pipeline −arch ev6 −tune ev6) increased the speed to 750 Mflops.

5.3   Software pipelining

In the subroutine lngth4 shown above, another dependency would be present if the instructions were performed exactly in the order in which they are given in the program. In each line, an element of the array a is first loaded and then input for the FMA. However, the result of the load is not immediately available, but only after one cycle on the IBM workstation we are considering (see Table 2.1). The real sequence of instructions looks as follows:

```
c first floating point unit, first cycle:
c do one FMA (both t1 and a0 are available in registers) and load a1
        t1=t1+a0*a0
        a1=a(j+1)

c first floating point unit, second cycle:
c do one FMA (both t2 and a1 are available in registers) and load a0 for
c next iteration of loop
        t2=t2+a1*a1
        a0=a(j+0+4)

c second floating point unit, first cycle:
c do one FMA (both t3 and a2 are available in registers) and load a3
        t3=t3+a2*a2
        a3=a(j+2)

c second floating point unit, second cycle:
c do one FMA (both t4 and a3 are available in registers) and load a2 for
c next iteration of loop
        t4=t4+a3*a3
        a2=a(j+1+4)
```

Arranging instructions in groups that can be executed together in one cycle, without stalls caused by dependencies, is called software pipelining. An attempt to do software pipelining is done by most compilers at high optimization levels. In easy cases, like our norm calculation, their attempt is usually successful. In more complicated cases, compilers can fail to generate optimally pipelined code. Trying to do software pipelining by hand can help in some circumstances. Software pipelining is less important on architectures with out-of-order execution, such as the SGI R10000, HP PA-8000, Compaq/DEC EV6, IBM Power3 and Intel's Pentium Pro. Since the processor can switch to another stream of operations (if available), pipeline stalls are reduced. Hence, it is less important for the programmer to find ways to arrange the instructions in the perfect order, even though an overall correct ordering increases the performance.

Software pipelining is particularly difficult on processors with deep pipelines and/or no FMA instruction, such as the Compaq/DEC EV6. On such architectures, software pipelining even simple loop structures can become difficult for a programmer and impossible for the compiler. In many cases, there is a close relationship between the optimal unrolling depth and the software pipelining scheme. In general, compilers cannot detect such relations. As an illustration, let us look at the BLAS routine DAXPY.

```
do i=1,n
  a(i)=a(i)+alpha*b(i)
enddo
```

By trying various compiler options with the f77 compiler V5.2, we were not able to achieve a performance higher than 120 Mflops on the EV6 (500 Mhz). The reason is that the compiler tried to unroll this loop to a depth of 4, which does not lead to good pipelining. In fact, unrolling to a depth of 12 leads to optimal software pipelining for this processor, as shown below.

```
do i=1,n-11-12,12

a(i+0)=s0
t8=t8*alpha
t0=b(i+12)
s4=s4+t4
s8=a(i+8)

a(i+1)=s1
t9=t9*alpha
t1=b(i+13)
s5=s5+t5
s9=a(i+9)

a(i+2)=s2
t10=t10*alpha
t2=b(i+14)
s6=s6+t6
s10=a(i+10)

a(i+3)=s3
t11=t11*alpha
```

```
t3=b(i+15)
s7=s7+t7
s11=a(i+11)

a(i+4)=s4
t0=t0*alpha
t4=b(i+16)
s8=s8+t8
s0=a(i+12)

a(i+5)=s5
t1=t1*alpha
t5=b(i+17)
s9=s9+t9
s1=a(i+13)

a(i+6)=s6
t2=t2*alpha
t6=b(i+18)
s10=s10+t10
s2=a(i+14)

a(i+7)=s7
t3=t3*alpha
t7=b(i+19)
s11=s11+t11
s3=a(i+15)

a(i+8)=s8
t4=t4*alpha
t8=b(i+20)
s0=s0+t0
s4=a(i+16)

a(i+9)=s9
t5=t5*alpha
t9=b(i+21)
s1=s1+t1
s5=a(i+17)

a(i+10)=s10
t6=t6*alpha
t10=b(i+22)
s2=s2+t2
s6=a(i+18)

a(i+11)=s11
t7=t7*alpha
t11=b(i+23)
s3=s3+t3
s7=a(i+19)

enddo
```

This hand-tuned version runs at 515 Mflops, even though the assembler listing shows that the compiler partially undid the optimal software pipelining. Coding everything in assembler would presumably lead to a slightly higher performance.

Nevertheless, this Fortran version is faster than the DAXPY routine found in the Compaq's DXML library, which runs at 430 Mflops.

Exercise: How many cycles separate dependent operations in the software-pipelined DAXPY code? Is this separation enough for optimality on the EV6 processor? (See Table 2.1.) Add a header and end section to this loop in such a way that the software-pipelined version gives the correct results for vectors of arbitrary length.

5.4 Improving the ratio of floating point operations to memory accesses

In addition to the advantages already discussed, loop unrolling can also be used to improve the ratio of floating point operations to loads/stores. This improved ratio can be beneficial for loops that have many array references. Such loops are dominated by memory accesses. Let us look at the following matrix-vector multiplication routine, multiplying the vector by the transposed matrix.

```
subroutine mult(n1,nd1,n2,nd2,y,a,x)
implicit real*8 (a-h,o-z)
dimension a(nd1,nd2),y(nd2),x(nd1)
do i=1,n2
  t=0.d0
  do j=1,n1
    t=t+a(j,i)*x(j)
  enddo
  y(i)=t
enddo
return
end
```

First, we note that the loop ordering is optimal from the point of view of data locality. All the memory accesses have unit stride. If the loop over i were the innermost one, the stride would be $nd1$ for accesses to a. The problem with this subroutine is that, even though the vector x has only $n1$ elements, we are loading $n1 \times n2$ elements of x. Expressed differently, each element of x is loaded $n2$ times. This is clearly a waste of memory bandwidth.

The subroutine "multo" shown below is an unrolled version of "mult." The effect demonstrated here is related to a better ratio of floating point to loads/stores in the optimized version "multo."

```
      subroutine multo(n1,nd1,n2,nd2,y,a,x)
c works correctly only if n1,n2 are multiples of 4
      implicit real*8 (a-h,o-z)
      dimension a(nd1,nd2),y(nd2),x(nd1)
      do i=1,n2-3,4
       t1=0.d0
       t2=0.d0
       t3=0.d0
       t4=0.d0
       do j=1,n1-3,4
```

```
      t1=t1+a(j+0,i+0)*x(j+0)+a(j+1,i+0)*x(j+1)+a(j+2,i+0)*x(j+2)+a(j+3,i+0)*x(j+3)
      t2=t2+a(j+0,i+1)*x(j+0)+a(j+1,i+1)*x(j+1)+a(j+2,i+1)*x(j+2)+a(j+3,i+1)*x(j+3)
      t3=t3+a(j+0,i+2)*x(j+0)+a(j+1,i+2)*x(j+1)+a(j+2,i+2)*x(j+2)+a(j+3,i+2)*x(j+3)
      t4=t4+a(j+0,i+3)*x(j+0)+a(j+1,i+3)*x(j+1)+a(j+2,i+3)*x(j+2)+a(j+3,i+3)*x(j+3)
    enddo
    y(i+0)=t1
    y(i+1)=t2
    y(i+2)=t3
    y(i+3)=t4
  enddo
  return
  end
```

In the case of the unoptimized version, two array elements $(a(j,i), x(j))$ have to be loaded into registers, resulting in two loads for one multiplication and one addition per loop iteration. In the unrolled case, 20 elements (16 elements of a, 4 of x) have to be loaded into registers, resulting in 20 loads for 16 multiplications and 16 additions. This effect is particularly important on machines that can do more floating point operations than loads in one cycle. At the same time, we have eliminated dependencies and better exposed the instruction parallelism. Timing on an IBM 590 workstation shows that, for the unoptimized version, one cycle is needed per loop iteration, whereas in the optimized version only .27 cycles are needed, corresponding to a speed of 240 Mflops. This impressive performance number cannot be explained solely by the eliminated dependencies and improved parallelism. If we had two loads per loop iteration, the best we could expect would be .8 cycles. Our earlier observation (Table 3.1) that the higher level BLAS routines perform better than the lower level ones is related to the fact that, by suitable loop unrolling, one can obtain a better floating point to load/store ratio for the higher level routines than for the lower level ones.

Exercise: Calculate the floating point to load/store ratio for a scalar product, a matrix times vector and a matrix times matrix multiplication for the case where all loops are unrolled to a depth of 3. Are there enough registers to unroll a matrix times matrix multiplication by a factor of 4 with respect to all indices?

In this simple case, loop unrolling was enough to obtain this speedup. Most compilers do a good job at unrolling when invoked at an appropriate optimization level. We actually verified this for both the IBM and SGI compilers.

Complex arithmetic has a better ratio of floating point operations to load/store operations. This is especially important for level-1 BLAS routines such as a ZAXPY. Therefore, complex arrays can and should be used wherever possible. If the language does not provide for complex data types, the real and imaginary parts should be adjacent in memory.

Exercise: Compare the floating point to load/store ratio for a real (DAXPY) and complex (ZAXPY) scalar product.

5.5   Running out of registers

Loop unrolling has turned out to be a useful tool in several contexts. But there
is a practical limit to the benefits that can be obtained from unrolling. Excessive
loop unrolling can even be detrimental to performance if it leads to running out
of registers. The content of the registers then has to be spilled back to the cache
for intermediate storage. The effect is an increased number of loads/stores. All of
the loops considered up to this point were very simple and short. In order to get
spilling, it would have been necessary to unroll them at large depths, such as 8 or 16.

For larger and more complicated inner loops, even unrolling to a depth of 2 could
lead to spilling. In such loops, the optimization techniques related to unrolling may
not be applicable, given the available number of registers. A look at the assembler
listing can reveal, and allow one to correct, problems caused by spilling. Using
compiler options that trigger automatic loop unrolling, without carefully monitoring
their effect, can lead to serious performance degradations. If the unrolled loop leads
to spilling, the remedy in some cases is to split the loop in two, a procedure called
loop fission. This can be done in a straightforward way only if two independent
code segments are present in the loop.

To a first approximation, the number of floating point registers needed in a loop
is equal to the number of floating point variables. A floating point variable can
either be a scalar variable or the element of an array. Frequently, a compiler is not
able to detect that a floating point variable is not reused within a basic block and
that therefore it would be possible to reuse the register for another floating point
variable. To illustrate this effect let us look at the subroutine "spill" below. In this
example, 32 array elements are loaded in one loop iteration and four scalar variables
are used to sum up the results. The compiler needs 36 floating point registers, four
more than are available.

```
subroutine spill(n,a,b,c,d,sum)
implicit real*8 (a-h,o-z)
dimension a(n),b(n),c(n),d(n)
suma=0.d0
sumb=0.d0
sumc=0.d0
sumd=0.d0
do 100,i=1,n-7,8
  suma=suma+a(i+0)+a(i+1)+a(i+2)+a(i+3)+a(i+4)+a(i+5)+a(i+6)+a(i+7)
  sumb=sumb+b(i+0)+b(i+1)+b(i+2)+b(i+3)+b(i+4)+b(i+5)+b(i+6)+b(i+7)
  sumc=sumc+c(i+0)+c(i+1)+c(i+2)+c(i+3)+c(i+4)+c(i+5)+c(i+6)+c(i+7)
  sumd=sumd+d(i+0)+d(i+1)+d(i+2)+d(i+3)+d(i+4)+d(i+5)+d(i+6)+d(i+7)
100     continue
sum=suma+sumb+sumc+sumd
return
end
```

However, the code could easily be rearranged in such a way that 12 registers are
enough. Assuming that all of the temporary variables, t1 to t8, are associated with
registers, the resulting instruction schedule is shown below. This schedule is just a
proof of principle, the point being that it is possible to find schedules that do not
lead to spilling. In practice, using more than 12 registers is usually desirable in
order to hide cache miss latency.

```
do 100,i=1,n-7,8
t1=a(i+0)
t2=a(i+1)
suma=suma+t1+t2
t3=b(i+0)
t4=b(i+1)
sumb=sumb+t3+t4
t5=c(i+0)
t6=c(i+1)
sumc=sumc+t5+t6
t7=d(i+0)
t8=d(i+1)
sumd=sumd+t7+t8
t1=a(i+2)
t2=a(i+3)
suma=suma+t1+t2
t3=b(i+2)
t4=b(i+3)
sumb=sumb+t3+t4
t5=c(i+2)
t6=c(i+3)
sumc=sumc+t5+t6
t7=d(i+2)
t8=d(i+3)
sumd=sumd+t7+t8
t1=a(i+4)
t2=a(i+5)
suma=suma+t1+t2
t3=b(i+4)
t4=b(i+5)
sumb=sumb+t3+t4
t5=c(i+4)
t6=c(i+5)
sumc=sumc+t5+t6
t7=d(i+4)
t8=d(i+5)
sumd=sumd+t7+t8
t1=a(i+6)
t2=a(i+7)
suma=suma+t1+t2
t3=b(i+6)
t4=b(i+7)
sumb=sumb+t3+t4
t5=c(i+6)
t6=c(i+7)
sumc=sumc+t5+t6
t7=d(i+6)
sumd=sumd+t7+t8
100 continue
sum=suma+sumb+sumc+sumd
```

Present compiler technology is not able to generate such an instruction schedule.
Even worse, for hand-optimized loops, such as the one shown above, the compiler
will undo these optimizations, actually producing the same inefficient code as in
the case of the original version of the loop. Looking at the assembler language
generated by the IBM xlf compiler, we identify five spilling loads and five spilling
stores, indicating that the compiler needs 37 instead of the estimated 36 registers.

In the C language it is possible to explicitly assign variables to registers, as shown below. Unfortunately this is only a hint to the compiler, and most compilers simply ignore such an assignment. Hence, we identify the same number of spills in the assembler code generated by the IBM xlc compiler (version 4.01) for the C code with explicit register assignments listed below.

The reason why all these hand optimizations are ignored is due to the instruction scheduling and register allocation phases of an optimizing compiler, described in section 3.5. It follows from the principles outlined there that the only possible way to prevent the compiler from reordering the hand-tuned instruction sequence across the whole loop body is to split the loop into several basic blocks. For instance, this can be done by introducing meaningless if-statements at strategic places. To avoid spending any cycles on these if-statements, they can later be taken out of the assembler code by hand. It would be much more desirable if the same effect were obtained by introducing some compiler directives, such as "begin basic block" and "end basic block." Unfortunately, no commercial compiler offers this possibility at the moment.

```
int spill(int *n, double *a, double *b, double *c, double *d, double *sum)
{
        int i;
        register double t1, t2, t3, t4, t5, t6, t7, t8, sum1, sum2, sum3, sum4;
        sum1 = 0.;
        sum2 = 0.;
        sum3 = 0.;
        sum4 = 0.;
        for (i = 0; i < (*n); i += 8) {
            t1 = a[i];
            t2 = a[i+1];
            sum1 = sum1 + t1 + t2;
            t3 = b[i];
            t4 = b[i+1];
            sum2 = sum2 + t3 + t4;
            t5 = c[i];
            t6 = c[i+1];
            sum3 = sum3 + t5 + t6;
            t7 = d[i];
            t8 = d[i+1];
            sum4 = sum4 + t7 + t8;

            etc ......
```

In some rare cases, slight spilling can be advantageous. This is the case only if the memory bandwidth is very poor. On an IBM 604 PowerPC, memory access operations for out of cache data take some 20 cycles, compared with only one cycle on the IBM Power2 architectures. The subroutine "mxvb," shown below, performs a matrix-vector multiplication for a matrix that is composed of 10×10 diagonal blocks, all of which contain the same matrix elements.

```
        subroutine mxvb(n,x,y)
        implicit real*8 (a-h,o-z)
        parameter (a1=2.d0,a2=3.d0,a3=4.d0,a4=5.d0,a5=6.d0,
    &   a6=7.d0,a7=8.d0,a8=9.d0,a9=10.d0,a10=11.d0)
```

```
dimension x(10,n),y(10,n)
do 200,i=1,n
  t1=0.d0
  t2=0.d0
  t3=0.d0
  t4=0.d0
  t5=0.d0
  t6=0.d0
  t7=0.d0
  t8=0.d0
  t9=0.d0
  t10=0.d0
  do 100,j=1,n
    t1=t1+a1*x(1,j)
    t2=t2+a2*x(2,j)
    t3=t3+a3*x(3,j)
    t4=t4+a4*x(4,j)
    t5=t5+a5*x(5,j)
    t6=t6+a6*x(6,j)
    t7=t7+a7*x(7,j)
    t8=t8+a8*x(8,j)
    t9=t9+a9*x(9,j)
    t10=t10+a10*x(10,j)
  100 continue
  y(1,i)=t1
  y(2,i)=t2
  y(3,i)=t3
  y(4,i)=t4
  y(5,i)=t5
  y(6,i)=t6
  y(7,i)=t7
  y(8,i)=t8
  y(9,i)=t9
  y(10,i)=t10
200    continue
  return
  end
```

In the subroutine mxvb, 30 floating point registers are needed. The array y has to be reloaded from memory in each outer loop iteration. Unrolling the inner loop to a depth of 2 leads to spilling, since 60 registers are needed. However, the number of times the array y has to be loaded is cut in half. If memory access is very slow, it can be advantageous, as shown in Table 5.1.

The example above may seem somewhat contrived. However, there are realistic loops where the situation is very similar. For fast Fourier transformations (FFTs) of very large data sets, the number of loads/stores can be cut in half by using radix 16 kernels instead of radix 4 kernels. The radix 16 kernels are very complex and will always lead to spilling.

Even though all of the current commercial RISC architectures have 32 floating point registers, not all the registers are always accessible to code operands. Some are reserved for special purposes. For high efficiency on a wide variety of machines, one should attempt to limit the number of scalar variables in a loop to approximately 28.

In this context it is also worthwhile pointing out that usually the number of physical registers is larger than the 32 logical registers we mentioned. On a proces-

Table 5.1: *The speed in Mflops for the subroutine mxvb listed above on an IBM* 590 *workstation and a PowerPC* 604 *for small data sets residing in cache and larger data sets that do not fit in cache. The behavior is very different due to the widely different access times for out of cache data.*

	590		604	
	In cache	Out of cache	In cache	Out of cache
Not unrolled	220	30	360	5
Unrolled	200	30	220	9

sor with a deep pipeline and with a long latency, all the logical registers associated with the operation could be occupied for the full duration of that instruction. By doing register renaming, these logical registers are freed after the initiation of the operation and the number of logical registers required is essentially the same as if the pipeline had a one-cycle depth.

In addition to the floating point registers, 32 integer registers are also present, utilized for integer arithmetic or for holding the addresses of array elements. According to our experience, the floating point registers normally spill ahead of the integer registers. Since utilization of integer registers is not a bottleneck, the topic will not be discussed in the book.

5.6 An example where automatic loop unrolling fails

As has been shown several times in various examples, loop unrolling is done by most compilers at the aggressive optimization levels. Judging from the success of the compilers in unrolling the simple loops presented so far, the reader might get the deceptive impression that modern compilers can do all needed optimizations. To rebut this impression, we will now present a rather easy loop structure where the IBM xlf (version 4.01) and SGI f77 compilers (MIPSpro_7.2.1) fail to do loop unrolling optimally.

```
      sum=0.d0
      do 100,j=1,n
      do 100,i=1,n
      sum=sum+x(i,j)*(i**2+j**2)
100   continue
```

The reason why the compilers fail to do the loop unrolling is that $i^2 + j^2$ depends on the loop indices. Nevertheless, it is easy to do the loop unrolling by hand, as shown below.

```
      subroutine sub2(n,x,sum)
      implicit real*8 (a-h,o-z)
      dimension x(n,n)
      sum1=0.d0
      sum2=0.d0
```

```
         sum3=0.d0
         sum4=0.d0
         rj=-1.d0
         sj=0.d0
         do 100,j=1,n-1,2
           rj=rj+2.d0
           sj=sj+2.d0
           rj2=rj*rj
           sj2=sj*sj
           ri=-1.d0
           si=0.d0
           do 100,i=1,n-1,2
             ri=ri+2.d0
             si=si+2.d0
             tt=rj2+ri*ri
             ss=rj2+si*si
             uu=sj2+ri*ri
             vv=sj2+si*si
             sum1=sum1+x(i,j)*tt
             sum2=sum2+x(i+1,j)*ss
             sum3=sum3+x(i,j+1)*uu
             sum4=sum4+x(i+1,j+1)*vv
100      continue
         sum=sum1+sum2+sum3+sum4
```

This hand-optimized version runs three times faster than the best compiler code generated from the unoptimized version. Note that in the hand-optimized version we have also eliminated type conversions from integers to floating point numbers by introducing the floating point variables ri, si, rj and sj, holding the floating point equivalents of i, $i+1$, j and $j+1$. However, this is a minor effect. Other examples where compiler-produced loop unrolling fails will be presented in section 9.4, where we look at a realistic program.

5.7   Loop unrolling overheads

Loop unrolling overheads can be substantial for multiple loop structures and small data sets. Most of the overhead comes from the tail section of each unrolled loop that is required for the correctness of the computation, for those cases where the number of loop iterations is not a multiple of the unrolling depth. It is therefore recommended, wherever possible, to choose the size of the data sets such that they are a multiple of the unrolling depth employed. In this way, unrolling by hand becomes easier and the performance goes up. Such a selection for the logical size of the data sets is not incompatible to choosing different leading dimensions for optimal cache use, as will be discussed in Chapter 6.

5.8   Aliasing

Two arrays, labeled by different names, are aliased if they refer to identical memory locations. The rules for allowing certain kinds of aliasing are different in various programming languages. Fortran severely restricts aliasing, whereas C allows it.

Hence, a Fortran compiler has more information than a C compiler and presumably can do a better optimizing job. In this section we will first explain the issues related to aliasing and then describe solutions for C and C++ programs.

Let us consider the following subroutine:

```
      subroutine sub(n,a,b,c,sum)
      implicit real*8 (a-h,o-z)
      dimension a(n),b(n),c(n)

      sum=0.d0
      do 100,i=1,n
        a(i)=b(i) + 2.d0*c(i)
        sum=sum + b(i)
100   continue

      return
      end
```

According to the Fortran rules, two dummy arguments cannot be aliased if either one of them is modified by the subroutine. When calling a subroutine with identical arguments, the compiler will usually tolerate it, but the results are unpredictable. Such a subroutine call is syntactically correct, but semantically incorrect. We show below a semantically incorrect call to the subroutine and a semantically correct call. We can imagine other scenarios leading to the same aliasing. For example, if we equivalenced the arrays a and b in the main program, the semantically correct sequence would become incorrect.

```
      implicit real*8 (a-h,o-z)
      parameter (n=1000)
      dimension a(n),b(n),c(n)

      do 10,i=1,n
        a(i)=1.d0
        b(i)=1.d0
        c(i)=2.d0
10    continue

      c semantically correct call
      call sub(n,a,b,c,sum)
      c semantically incorrect call
      call sub(n,a,a,c,sum)
```

As we have learned already, most compilers do software pipelining. There are many possible ways to software-pipeline the subroutine sub. One such possibility is shown below, in Fortran. For simplicity, let us assume that we are running on hardware capable of performing one floating point operation and one load or store per cycle. Let us also assume that the depth of the floating point unit is two stages for a fused floating point multiplication-addition; i.e., the result is only available two cycles after the operation started. The latency of load/store operations is one cycle. Under these assumptions, all the groups in the code below separated by comments, containing one or two instructions, can be performed in consecutive cycles. This is due to the fact that dependent groups are separated by at least one cycle. Therefore, only three cycles are needed to complete one loop iteration. As expected, the correct result is obtained using the semantically correct calling sequence. If the instructions are executed exactly in the order shown below, an incorrect result is obtained in the case of the semantically incorrect calling sequence. This is due to the fact that the old elements of b are used to form the sum, instead of the updated ones.

```
        tb=b(1)
        tc=c(1)
        do 100,i=1,n-1

c first cycle
            ta=tb+2.d0*tc
            tc=c(i+1)

c second cycle
            sum=sum+tb
            tb=b(i+1)

c third cycle
            a(i)=ta

100        continue
            i=n
            ta=tb+2.d0*tc
            sum=sum+tb
            a(i)=ta
```

Let us now consider a second possible way to schedule the instructions, as shown below. In this case the software pipelining is not optimal. In order to resolve the dependencies, we introduce an idle cycle, denoted by NOOP. Moreover, the floating point addition is not overlapped with a load/store. This loop iteration takes eight cycles, instead of three cycles in the software-pipelined version. As the reader can verify, this nonoptimal instruction schedule gives the correct result for both the semantically correct and the semantically incorrect Fortran calling sequences. Even though "NOOP" is not a Fortran instruction, we have mixed it with conventional Fortran syntax.

```
        do 100,i=1,n
          tc=c(i)
          tb=b(i)
          ta=tb+2.d0*tc
          NOOP
          a(i)=ta
          tb=b(i)
          sum=sum+tb
100        continue
```

An important point is that a semantically incorrect structure in Fortran is perfectly correct in standard C or C++. According to the ANSI C standard, any two variables of the same type (such as integers or double precision numbers) can be aliased. This means that the compiler always has to assume the worst-case scenario, the one in which severe aliasing is present. This is confirmed by looking at the assembler code generated by the IBM C compiler for the corresponding C version of the program. The instruction schedule generated is essentially identical to the one shown above. Obviously, the standard C conventions prevent the compiler from doing efficient, software-pipelined, instruction scheduling. The execution time of the C program on an IBM 550 workstation is eight cycles per loop iteration, compared to three cycles per iteration for the Fortran code.

In the example above we concentrated only on the relatively simple case where $a(i)$ was equivalenced to $b(i)$. More complicated aliasing schemes are possible in C, such as $a(i)$ being equivalenced to $b(i + 2)$. Scalar variables could also be aliased to certain array elements, such as $a(9)$ being equivalenced to sum.

Most C compilers allow for compiler options or compiler directives that declare aliasing to be illegal. The details are vendor specific and can be found in the man pages or users' manual. If these options are used, a C code should, in principle, be as fast as the corresponding Fortran code. The C compiler then has the same information and should be able to do essentially the same optimizations. In practice, though, this is not always the case. Another way to alleviate the performance penalty associated with aliasing is to assign by hand all array elements that are not subject to aliasing to different local scalar variables. In this way, the compiler can perform beneficial optimizations.

Even though aliasing problems exist mainly in C, they can also be found in Fortran, when indirectly indexed arrays or pointers are used. Let us look at an example involving indirectly indexed arrays.

```
      subroutine sub(n,a,b,ind)
      implicit real*8 (a-h,o-z)
      dimension a(n),b(n),ind(n)

      do 100,i=1,n
        b(ind(i))=1.d0+2.d0*b(ind(i))+3.d0*a(i)
100   continue

      return
      end
```

Evidently, consecutive loop iterations are not independent if $ind(i) = ind(i + 1)$. Fortran compilers have to take this possibility into account and therefore turn off software pipelining which involves working on several independent loop iterations simultaneously. Some compilers allow for the use of directives indicating that $ind(i)$ is an invertible mapping and hence aliasing is not present.

Pointers are a standard in Fortran90 and are also available in some Fortran77 implementations. They make up another feature that can lead to aliasing ambiguities. We will illustrate this effect for the sample Fortran90 program shown below that updates the positions of a set of n particles using their velocities. As discussed earlier in section 3.3, the ideal data structure would be one where the x, y and z components of all the arrays are adjacent in memory. In this example, we assume that the three components are in different arrays. Since the different elements of the position and the velocity are referenced by pointers only in the subroutine "move," the compiler has to allow for the possibility that they are aliased. The generated code may not be efficient. Any arithmetic operation has to be preceded directly by the loads of all the operands involved and followed by an immediate store of the result. On an IBM Power2 architecture, this also prevents the compiler from issuing double load and store instructions that can do the load of the ith and $(i + 1)$th component of the x component of the velocity in a single cycle. The reason for this is that, if the $(i + 1)$th component of the velocity was aliased to the ith component of the position, a wrong result would be obtained.

```
MODULE declarations
        type position_type
                double precision, dimension(:), pointer :: rx, ry, rz
        end type position_type
        type velocity_type
                double precision, dimension(:), pointer :: vx, vy, vz
        end type velocity_type
END MODULE declarations

PROGRAM test
        USE declarations
        implicit none
        integer :: n
        type(position_type) :: position
        type(velocity_type) :: velocity

        n=1000
        ALLOCATE(position%rx(n),position%ry(n),position%rz(n))
        ALLOCATE(velocity%vx(n),velocity%vy(n),velocity%vz(n))
        position%rx=0.d0; position%ry=0.d0; position%rz=0.d0
        velocity%vx=1.d0; velocity%vy=1.d0; velocity%vz=1.d0

        call move(n,position,velocity)

END PROGRAM

        SUBROUTINE move(n,position,velocity)
        USE declarations
        implicit none
        integer :: i,n
        type(position_type) position
        type(velocity_type) velocity
        double precision, parameter :: dt=1.d-1

        do i=1,n-1,2
          position%rx(i)=position%rx(i)+dt*velocity%vx(i)
          position%ry(i)=position%ry(i)+dt*velocity%vy(i)
          position%rz(i)=position%rz(i)+dt*velocity%vz(i)
          position%rx(i+1)=position%rx(i+1)+dt*velocity%vx(i+1)
          position%ry(i+1)=position%ry(i+1)+dt*velocity%vy(i+1)
          position%rz(i+1)=position%rz(i+1)+dt*velocity%vz(i+1)
        enddo

        END SUBROUTINE move
```

5.9   Array arithmetic in Fortran90

In addition to pointers, mentioned in the previous section, there are many other features in Fortran90 that may make it slower than Fortran77. One such feature is array syntax, which avoids explicit loop structures. In this section we will give a few examples of Fortran90 array syntax structure leading to poor performance.

Let us look at the following Fortran77 loop, where the positions of a collection of particles are propagated along the path determined by their velocities.

```
        do 100,i=1,n
          rxyz(1,i)=rxyz(1,i)+vxyz(1,i)*dt
          rxyz(2,i)=rxyz(2,i)+vxyz(2,i)*dt
          rxyz(3,i)=rxyz(3,i)+vxyz(3,i)*dt
100     continue
```

Assuming the arrays involved are dimensioned $(3, n)$, the same loop can be written with Fortran90 array syntax as

```
        rxyz=rxyz+vxyz*dt
```

Obviously, the compiler has a much more difficult task now. In Fortran77, the loop ordering was fixed and the short inner loop unrolled. In Fortran90, the compiler has to figure out all these settings. The IBM xlf compiler (version 5.01) generates optimal code when invoked with the option "$-O3$ $-$qhot." In this case the performance is identical to the Fortran77 loops; otherwise it is three times slower. The Cray compiler (cf90 3.4.0.0) did a very good job on these loops. Even though it came up with different solutions depending on how the loops were presented, all the compiler-generated code led to high performance. This compiler either automatically chose the loop over the three spatial components as the inner loop and unrolled it, or it first collapsed the loop over the particles with the loop over the spatial components and then unrolled the single resulting loop to a depth of 4.

One compromise, allowing the expression of this computation in a more compact form than in the Fortran 77 explicit loops, is shown below. The IBM Fortran90 compiler does a good job at optimizing this loop, although this may not be true for other available compilers.

```
        do 100,i=1,n
          rxyz(:,i)=rxyz(:,i)+vxyz(:,i)*dt
100     continue
```

Let us next look at Fortran90 matrix functions. The three-loop structure that is necessary in Fortran77 to specify a matrix multiplication can be compactly expressed in Fortran90 as

```
        c=matmul(a,b)
```

Again, the compiler has a much more difficult task now. In Fortran77, the programmer has to specify the ordering of the three loops necessary for a matrix multiplication. Unless a very high optimization level was used for the compilation, the compiler will not change this loop ordering. In Fortran90, the compiler has to find the loop ordering itself. As it turns out, compilers frequently fail to generate optimal code in these cases. If performance is necessary and the Fortran90 functions do not deliver fast code, the alternative is to use optimized math libraries instead. For the specific case of matrix operations from the BLAS library, this replacement

can be done automatically by using specialized libraries such as the following:
(http://www.nag.co.uk/numeric/F95_BLAS_Proposal/F95_BLAS_Proposal.html).
The Cray compiler does this replacement automatically.

Things get even worse when more complicated array syntax expressions are
utilized, such as

```
c=matmul(a,a)+matmul(a,matmul(a,a))
```

Many compilers will not recognize that a common subexpression is present, namely
"matmul(a,a)," but instead will calculate it twice. This results not only in a performance loss, but also in the allocation of two temporary arrays instead of just one,
increasing memory consumption. The performance loss can be partially avoided by
defining a work array b and pulling out the common subexpression:

```
b=matmul(a,a)
c=b+matmul(a,b)
```

However, this may not be as fast as the two corresponding BLAS calls. On a Com-
paq/DEC EV6 with the compiler version 5.2 this code took 12 seconds to execute
for a 1000 by 1000 matrix, while the BLAS routine only took 6.3 seconds. The
Fortran90 timing was obtained by compiling the program with the highest optimization level "−O5." At the optimization level −O2, the Fortran90 performance
was 20 times lower. In this example the Cray compiler failed to replace the Fortran
matrix function by a call to the BLAS library. This compiler identifies the pattern
"c=c+matmul(a,b)" but not "c=b+matmul(a,b)." In order to have the replacement done automatically with the CRAY compiler cf90 3.4.0.0, the code has to be
rearranged in the following way:

```
b=matmul(a,a)
c=b
c=c+matmul(a,b)
```

Finally, let's look in greater detail at an example that was extensively discussed
in section 5.2, the calculation of the norm of a vector. In Fortran90 this may be
written compactly as

```
s=sum(a*a)
```

On an IBM 590 workstation, this code leads to a performance of just 45 Mflops,
whereas the Fortran77 version ran at 260 Mflops. The reason for the low Fortran90
performance is that most compilers will first define a work array whose ith element
is the square of the ith of a and then do the summation in a second step. Again,
not only performance but also memory is wasted. This example was chosen as an
illustration. In practice, this operation would be performed by calling the Fortran90
function dot_product(a,a). However, as discussed above, the intrinsic function often
has lower performance than that of the BLAS DDOT routine.

From a performance point of view the conclusion is now clear. Given the state
of the affairs in Fortran90 compiler technology, Fortran90 code is likely to lead
to lower performance than Fortran77. One workaround is by using Fortran77 or
specialized libraries in the hotspots of Fortran90 programs. Our tests also revealed
that several Fortran90 compilers have reliability problems. The Cray compiler was
an exception in that respect.

5.10   Operator overloading in C++

Object-oriented languages, such as C++ and to a certain extent Fortran90, have many features that might be helpful to a programmer, but that are frequently detrimental to performance. In the preceding section we already discussed such a feature for Fortran90. Here we will concentrate on operator overloading, which allows the assignment of several meanings to one symbol in object-oriented languages. The meaning is chosen depending on the context. For instance, we could overload the summation sign, "+." If it is found between two scalars, it has the conventional effect, while if it is used with two vectors, it will add these two vectors element by element. If three vectors are added,

        x = a + b + c

a temporary vector is allocated dynamically to hold the intermediate result $a + b$, which is then added to c in a second step. The number of memory accesses is considerably increased, in addition to the overhead for the allocation of the temporary arrays. The performance problem is even more serious than in the case of Fortran90 array arithmetic, since the operations are described by external (user-written or library) functions, whereas in Fortran90 intrinsic functions are utilized. Template libraries that can overcome some of these limitations have recently become available (http://oonumerics.org/blitz/).

5.11   Elimination of floating point exceptions

A floating point operation where the operand is outside an allowed range leads to a "floating point exception." The way in which the operating system (OS) of computers from different vendors handles floating point exceptions varies, despite the existence of IEEE standards in this regard. On some computers, execution stops on floating point exceptions, while others return nonnumeric values. Taking the square root of a negative number might return "NaNQ" or "nan," dividing by zero "INF." Such floating point exceptions cause pipeline stalls that significantly degrade performance. While results of this type are in many cases an indication that something went wrong in the program, they could also be a consequence of some optimized array structures. For instance, padding an array whose dimensions are a multiple of a power of 2 with additional elements in order to avoid cache thrashing is a widely utilized technique. Looping over all the array elements with operations such as square roots can result in floating point exceptions if the padded elements take on values incompatible with the operation. For increased performance, necessary precautions need to be taken to keep floating point exceptions to a strict minimum.

5.12   Type conversions

Type conversions, such as the conversion of a floating point number to an integer or vice versa, are costly since they usually involve several instructions possibly executed in different functional units of the processor. Incrementing an integer should therefore be written as

```
i = i + 1
```

instead of

```
i = i + 1.
```

avoiding the conversion of the floating point number "1." into the integer "1." Similarly, incrementing a floating point number by 1 should be written as

```
r = s + 1.
```

instead of

```
r = s + 1
```

In particular, mixing of single and double precision numbers in a single expression should be avoided. When using double precision arithmetic, this can happen easily because many compilers consider a number of the form "1." as a single precision number. In such a case, explicitly writing "1.d0" instead will cure the problem. For floating point numbers, some compilers will actually do the conversion at compile time. In this case, the only degradation is numerical, related to the loss of accuracy when mixing single precision numbers in double precision expressions.

One exception where integer and floating point numbers should be mixed is the calculation of exponentials. The line

```
r = s**2.d0
```

will result in a costly call to the intrinsic power function (see section 5.15), whereas

```
r = s**2
```

will be replaced (section 3.5) by a simple multiplication ($r = s*s$).

5.13   Sign conversions

Sign conversions are expensive operations. As an example, three cycles are needed on the IBM Power architecture. Hiding sign conversions in consecutive floating point operations can give results that are not bitwise identical. Therefore, such transformations are not done by compilers at medium optimization levels. This line of code

```
a(i)=-(1.d0-.5d0*b(i))
```

will execute slower than the following one, where the superfluous sign conversion instruction is eliminated:

```
a(i)=-1.d0+.5d0*b(i)
```

On IBM machines, the compiler will do this transformation at the highest optimization level "−O3" and print the warning message "Optimization level 3 has the potential to alter the semantics of a program."

5.14   Complex arithmetic

Fortran provides for the usage of complex data type. Complex linear algebra operations are beneficial to performance due to their improved ratio of floating point operations to load/store operations (section 5.4). The performance obtained in this case is, in general, independent of whether the operations are coded using complex or real data type. However, if loops involve operations that go beyond additions and multiplications, it is frequently advantageous to formulate the complex arithmetic using real data type. Such a subroutine is shown below.

```
      subroutine sub1(n,a,b,tt)
      implicit real*8 (a-h,o-z)
      complex a,b
      dimension a(n),b(n)

      do i=1,n-3,4
        a(i+0)= conjg(b(i+0))*tt
        a(i+1)= conjg(b(i+1))*tt
        a(i+2)= conjg(b(i+2))*tt
        a(i+3)= conjg(b(i+3))*tt
      enddo

      return
      end
```

By using real data type in this subroutine, a sign conversion can be avoided. On an IBM Power2 architecture, a 30% speedup results.

```
      subroutine sub2(n,a,b,tt)
      dimension a(2,n),b(2,n)
      implicit real*8 (a-h,o-z)

      tm=-tt
      do i=1,n-3,4
        a(1,i+0)= b(1,i+0)*tt
        a(2,i+0)= b(2,i+0)*tm
        a(1,i+1)= b(1,i+1)*tt
        a(2,i+1)= b(2,i+1)*tm
        a(1,i+2)= b(1,i+2)*tt
        a(2,i+2)= b(2,i+2)*tm
        a(1,i+3)= b(1,i+3)*tt
        a(2,i+3)= b(2,i+3)*tm
      enddo

      return
      end
```

5.15   Special functions

The calculation of special functions, such as divisions, square roots, exponentials and logarithms requires anywhere from a few dozen cycles up to hundreds of cycles. This is due to the fact that these calculations have to be decomposed into a sequence of elementary instructions such as multiplies and adds. Table 5.2 shows the number

Table 5.2: *Number of cycles needed for the calculation of double precision special functions on several processors. DPOWER denotes the operation x^y. These timings should only be taken as an approximate indication of the cost to compute special functions. The actual timing depends on the value of the input argument. We have included the Cray libbench library and the vector version of the IBM MASS library as examples of libraries that are faster at the cost of a slightly decreased accuracy.*

Processor	DIVIDE	DSQRT	DSIN	DEXP	DLOG	DPOWER
IBM RS/6000 P2	20	30	51	54	52	179
IBM RS/6000 P2 (MASS)		7	12	6	8	65
Cray T3E	30	82	133	87	149	780
Cray T3E (libbench)		32	46	34	33	62
SGI R10000	21	36	125	119	110	257

of cycles required for some common special functions on several processors. The first advice is to keep the number of special function calls to a strict minimum. The number of special function calls can sometimes be reduced by storing the values of repeatedly used arguments in an array, instead of recalculating them every time. Frequently, usage of mathematical identities can reduce the number of special function evaluations. For example, calculating $\log(x*y)$ is nearly two times faster than calculating $\log(x) + \log(y)$.

A large fraction of the CPU time in the evaluation of special functions goes into the calculation of the last few bits. Relaxing accuracy demands has the potential of considerably speeding up these calculations. Most vendors have libraries that calculate special functions with slightly reduced accuracy, but significantly faster. Table 5.2 gives some representative timings for the Cray Libbench and the IBM MASS library that is available on the Web at http://www.rs6000.ibm.com/resource/technology/MASS. Further gains in speed can be obtained by using vectorized versions that are contained in some of these libraries, such as in the MASS library. Their use necessitates the calculation of many special functions simultaneously. Given a vector x of length 500 containing the input arguments, a call of the form

```
call VEXP(y,x,500)
```

will calculate the 500 exponentials and write them into y.

Concerning divisions, some compilers have options allowing to override the IEEE accuracy standards and to replace divisions by the faster sequence of an inverse and a multiply (for instance, the "IEEE_arithmetic" flag with SGI compilers).

By using information about the context in which the special functions are called or about the values their arguments take, it is often possible to write your own, faster version of a special function. Let us look at an example taken from an electronic structure code. The goal here is to calculate the potential vxc from the charge density rho on all grid points in a three-dimensional structure. Neglecting all multiplicative factors, the potential is $rho^{\frac{1}{3}}$. A simplified version of the subroutine is shown below.

```
      subroutine xc(n1,n2,n3,rho,vxc)
      implicit real*8 (a-h,o-z)
      dimension rho(n1,n2,n3),vxc(n1,n2,n3)
      do 10,i3=1,n3
      do 10,i2=1,n2
      do 10,i1=1,n1
        vxc(i1,i2,i3)=rho(i1,i2,i3)**.33333333333333d0
10    continue
      return
      end
```

It is well known that $rho^{\frac{1}{3}}$ can be calculated by finding the root of the function $f(vxc) = vxc^3 - rho$. By using Newton's method to find the zero, we introduce the iteration $vxc \leftarrow vxc - \frac{1}{3}(vxc - rho/vxc^2)$. A similar procedure is used in the standard libraries to calculate $rho^{\frac{1}{3}}$; as a result, it would be difficult to outperform them for arbitrary cases. However, in this special case we have additional information based on our understanding of the physical problem. We know that the charge density rho varies little from one grid point to another. Consequently, the potential varies little as well. This implies that the solution from a neighboring grid point is an excellent initial guess for the Newton iteration on the current point. Thus, we can significantly reduce the number of iterations compared to the case where no particularly good initial guess exists. In addition, one can assume that this small variation of the charge density along the x direction is similar for a group of four points along the y direction. Therefore, the number of Newton iterations required for these four points should be similar as well. This means that we check the fulfillment of the accuracy criterion for these four points in a combined way, thus reducing the number of if statements. The optimized version of the subroutine, based on these observations, is shown below. In a typical application, this version is five times faster than the unoptimized one.

```
      subroutine xc(n1,n2,n3,rho,vxc)
      implicit real*8 (a-h,o-z)
      dimension rho(n1,n2,n3),vxc(n1,n2,n3)
      x1=1.d0
      x2=1.d0
      x3=1.d0
      x4=1.d0
      do 10,i3=1,n3
      do 10,i2=1,n2-3,4
      do 10,i1=1,n1
        rhou1=rho(i1,i2+0,i3)
        rhou2=rho(i1,i2+1,i3)
        rhou3=rho(i1,i2+2,i3)
        rhou4=rho(i1,i2+3,i3)
15    continue
      d1=x1-rhou1/x1**2
      d2=x2-rhou2/x2**2
      d3=x3-rhou3/x3**2
      d4=x4-rhou4/x4**2
      x1=x1-.333333333333333d0*d1
      x2=x2-.333333333333333d0*d2
      x3=x3-.333333333333333d0*d3
      x4=x4-.333333333333333d0*d4
```

```
      if (d1**2+d2**2+d3**2+d4**2.gt.1.d-20) goto 15
        vxc(i1,i2+0,i3)=x1
        vxc(i1,i2+1,i3)=x2
        vxc(i1,i2+2,i3)=x3
        vxc(i1,i2+3,i3)=x4
10    continue

      return
      end
```

5.16   Eliminating overheads

This section will give some guidelines on how to estimate the cost of various overheads present in any scientific code and on how to keep these overheads to a strict minimum. We loosely use the word *overhead* here to indicate the cost incurred by nonarithmetic instructions.

5.16.1   If statements

If-statements slow down a program for several reasons. First, the compiler can do fewer optimizations in their presence, such as loop unrolling. Second, the evaluation of the conditional takes time by itself. Third, the continuous flow of data through the pipeline is interrupted when branching. The time for executing the branch condition itself is actually negligible and/or overlapped by other instructions. In many cases, if-statements can be significantly reduced or even eliminated completely by restructuring the program. This restructuring is very context dependent, so that it is difficult to provide general guidelines on how to do it. We will just present some examples for illustration.

Let us look at the following program calculating the number of elements *ic* in an array that needs to be summed up until its norm gets bigger than a threshold *thresh*; i.e., it searches for the smallest *ic* such that $\sqrt{\sum_{j=1}^{ic} a(j)^2} \geq thresh$.

```
      subroutine thresh0(n,a,thresh,ic)
      implicit real*8 (a-h,o-z)
      dimension a(n)

      ic=0
      tt=0.d0
      do 100,j=1,n
      tt=tt+a(j)*a(j)
      if (sqrt(tt).ge.thresh) then
        ic=j
        return
      endif
100   continue

      return
      end
```

In this case, the evaluation of the if statement is very expensive since it requires the calculation of a square root. The evaluation of the if statement can be simplified by squaring the two quantities to be compared, as shown below. Because of the finite precision arithmetic, transformations of this type are not always strictly equivalent to the original version. An if statement of the form "if (x1.lt.x2 .and. sqrt(x1).eq.sqrt(x2))" can be "true" in finite precision arithmetic for certain values of $x1$ and $x2$, whereas the condition would always be "false" in infinite precision. In applications, slight differences between two possible variants of an if statement, related to roundoff, are usually negligible. It is recommended, though, to use the same variant consistently throughout a program to avoid problems that might arise from such inconsistencies.

```
subroutine thresh1(n,a,thresh,ic)
implicit real*8 (a-h,o-z)
dimension a(n)

threshsq=thresh**2
ic=0
tt=0.d0
do 100,j=1,n
  tt=tt+a(j)*a(j)
  if (tt.ge.threshsq) then
    ic=j
    return
  endif
100   continue

return
end
```

This simple transformation of the conditional speeds up the routine by a factor of nearly 10 on an IBM 590. Nevertheless, further optimizations are still possible. If we took out all the code related to the if statement, we would retrieve the subroutine length from section 5.2. We remember that this routine ran at close to peak speed when compiled with the highest optimization or when hand tuned. If compiled with the $-O$ flag on an IBM 590, subroutine thresh1 runs at a sustained speed of only 10 Mflops. The reason for this low performance can be understood by looking at the pseudoassembler code shown below. We remember that one iteration of the loop took half a cycle in the optimized "length" routine, whereas it now takes 13 cycles. The evaluation of the if-condition (fcmpu and cror in the assembler code) alone takes 9 cycles. In addition, there is no loop unrolling. When compiled with the $-O3$ flag, the compiler partially succeeds in doing loop unrolling and the speed goes up to 55 Mflops.

```
40| 000038 lfdu    CC240008   2   LFDU    fp1,gr4=a(gr4,8)
40| 00003C fma     FC01007A   1   FMA     fp0=fp0,fp1,fp1,fcr
41| 000040 fcmpu   FC001000   3   CFL     cr0=fp0,fp2
41| 000044 cror    4CC11382   6   CR_0    cr1=cr[00],0x4/eq,0x40/fgt,0x80/feq
41| 000048 bc      4200FFE8   0   BCT     ctr=CL.27,taken=50%
41| 00004C bc      4186000C   0   BT      CL.10,cr1,0x4/eq ,taken=50%
45| 000050 ai      30630001   1   AI      gr3=gr3,1
```

This performance is still unsatisfactory, as the if statement still slows down the routine by nearly a factor of 5. Can we do better? When the vectors a are fairly long, as is usually the case, we expect that the threshold condition is met only after summing up lots of array elements, say, a few hundred. In this case, we can first sum up groups of 128 array elements before checking the threshold condition. If the condition is not yet met, we sum up the next bunch. If it is met, we go back through the last 128 elements individually to find out exactly where the condition was fulfilled. This is illustrated in the subroutine "thresh3" below.

```
          subroutine thresh3(n,a,thresh,ic)
          implicit real*8 (a-h,o-z)
          parameter(lot=128)
          dimension a(n)

          threshsq=thresh**2
          ic=0
          t1=0.d0
          t2=0.d0
          t3=0.d0
          t4=0.d0
          do 100,j=1,n-lot+1,lot
            do 55,i=0,lot-1-3,4
              t1=t1+a(j+i+0)**2
              t2=t2+a(j+i+1)**2
              t3=t3+a(j+i+2)**2
              t4=t4+a(j+i+3)**2
55          continue
            tt=t1+t2+t3+t4
            if (tt.ge.threshsq) then
              do 110,i=lot-1,0,-1
                tt=tt-a(j+i)**2
                if (tt.lt.threshsq) then
                  ic=j+i
                  return
                endif
110           continue
            endif
100       continue

          return
          end
```

This subroutine now runs at 180 Mflops. The parameter *lot* has to be chosen relative to the size of the array a and to the expected value of *ic*. If we anticipate that many thousands of array elements need to be summed up before satisfying the threshold condition, we choose *lot* = 1024, further improving the performance.

Let us look at a second example. While in the first example we just reduced the number of if statement evaluations, we will eliminate them completely in the example shown below.

```
          do 100,j=-n,n
          do 100,i=-n,n
            if (i**2+j**2.ne.0) then
            pot(i,j)=rho(i,j)/(i**2+j**2)
            else
            pot(i,j)=0.d0
            endif
100       continue
```

The if statement here is inserted just to prevent a division by zero when $i = j = 0$. Since the penalty for the if statement is high, and since the event causing the floating point exception occurs rarely, we should try to eliminate the if statement.

One possibility would be to split up both loops into three pieces, where the indices take on the values $-n$ to -1, 0 and 1 to n. Besides making the code longer, this scheme would be detrimental to performance since the loop lengths are short and loop overheads could become important. A better solution is to accept a division by zero for the case where $i = j = 0$. As discussed in section 5.11, the division by zero will be much slower than a division by a nonzero number since it leads to an exception handling. However, as it only happens once for n^2 divisions, this is really negligible. When done looping, we then just set the correct value of the element pot $(0,0)$. As discussed in section 5.6, loops of this type are frequently not optimized by the compiler. We have to use hand-optimization techniques discussed in the previous sections to achieve the highest possible performance level.

Exercise: Hand-optimize the loop structure discussed above.

After simplifying and/or reducing the number of if statements within important loops to a strict minimum, some conditionals will still remain in place. The ordering of those if statements can influence the performance. The subroutine "sub5," shown below, runs at different speeds on processors without branch prediction, depending on whether all the array elements of ll are set to "true" or "false," even though the total workload is exactly the same in both cases.

```
          subroutine sub5(n,a,ll,tt)
          implicit real*8 (a-h,o-z)
          logical ll
          dimension a(n),ll(n)

          tt=0.d0
          do 100,j=1,n
            if (ll(j)) then
              tt=tt+a(j)*a(j)
            else
              tt=tt-a(j)*a(j)
            endif
100       continue

          return
          end
```

Unfortunately there is no general rule as to which ordering is the most advantageous (Table 5.3). On IBM machines, programs usually run faster if the "true" condition comes first. On SGI R10000s, a processor with branch prediction, we found varying behavior, depending on the compiler utilized. In general, on a processor with branch prediction capabilities, such as the Compaq/DEC EV6, the order should not matter since the processor should presumably predict the right path of the branch. On such a processor the code should run slower for a mixture of "true" and "false" conditions, since it is no longer possible to predict the path taken by all branch statements.

Table 5.3: *The performance in Mflops of the subroutine "sub5," listed above, on various computers. The IBM Power2 395 is the only processor without branch prediction capabilities. Among the processors with branch prediction, only the EV6 shows the expected behavior, whereas both the IBM Power PC and the SGI R10000 of the Onyx show varying behavior. The performance data are given for the case where all elements of ll are set to the value "true," "false" and to a mixture of both.*

	IBM Pwr2 395	SGI Onyx	SGI Origin	IBM PwrPC 604	DEC EV6
"True"	100	40	70	110	245
Mixture	95	60	70	90	150
"False"	90	110	70	125	245

5.16.2   Loop overheads

Loops involve certain overheads. Registers needed within the loop must be freed by storing their old values in memory. Other registers containing loop counters and addresses have to be set. The exit from the loops necessarily involves a mispredicted branch. The resulting overhead can vary from a few up to a few dozen cycles. Such overhead is obviously negligible if a lot of work is done within the loop, either because one iteration of the loop involves a lot of numerical operations or because many iterations through the loop are present. In addition to the overhead, a second reason for the poor performance of short loops is their inefficient unrolling. If a loop that is unrolled to a depth of 4 is iterated six times, one-third of the operations are done in the unrolled end section. In addition, there is an additional overhead to be paid for the unrolling itself, as was previously explained.

While in many cases the loop length is fixed by external constraints, certain optimizations are sometimes possible. For a loop structure of the type

```
        do 100,i=1,n
        do 100,j=1,m
        ............
100     continue
```

n loop overheads are needed to set up the inner loop and one for the outer loop. If n is larger than m, it is better to switch the order of the loops

```
        do 100,j=1,m
        do 100,i=1,n
        ............
100     continue
```

since in this case the overall loop overhead is lower. However, as will be emphasized in the next chapter, the most important consideration in decisions related to loop ordering are those related to data locality. Of course, achieving both data locality and minimal loop overheads is the best of all worlds. In many cases this can be obtained by laying out data structures in such a way that the long dimensions of an array are to the left (in Fortran) or to the right (in C). An exception to this rule is when arrays have extremely short lengths (such as 2) in some dimensions and the loops are unrolled with respect to that index. That index should then be placed leftmost, with the longest dimension placed to its right.

```
dimension a(2,1000,50)
```

Sometimes it is possible to merge two loops into a single loop. A matrix copy routine such as

```
        dimension a(n,m)
        ........
        do 100,j=1,m
        do 100,i=1,n
          a(i,j)=b(i,j)
100     continue
```

runs slower than its one-dimensional vector equivalent

```
        dimension a(n*m)
        ........
        do 100,i=1,n*m
          a(i)=b(i)
100     continue
```

In many cases the compiler will do such a loop transformation, called loop collapsing, automatically.

Even though loop overheads are not entirely negligible, loops are far more efficient than corresponding "while" and "goto" constructs. Since loops are essential in the structure of any program, there is special hardware and software to execute loops as fast as possible. "Goto" and "while" structures cannot take advantage of such special features unless they are converted to their corresponding loops by the compiler.

5.16.3 Subroutine calling overheads

Subroutine calls incur overheads for the same reasons as loops do. The overhead depends on such things as the number of arguments that are passed and whether the routine itself calls other routines or not. The measured overhead on an IBM 590 for calling the simple subroutine below was 10 cycles, comparable to the loop overhead for a simple loop.

```
        subroutine fma(sum,x1,x2)
        implicit real*8 (a-h,o-z)
        sum=sum+x1*x2
        return
        end
```

The overhead for simple Fortran function calls is very similar. For very complex subroutine calls, overheads of 100 cycles or more are possible.

Subroutine calling overheads can be eliminated by a technique called inlining. The body of the called subroutine or function is inserted into the calling program. This can be done by invoking certain compiler options. If the subroutine to be inlined contains many lines of code, inlining can considerably increase the size of the whole program and lead to storage and other performance problems (see section 7.2).

5.17   Copy overheads in Fortran90

In Fortran90, it is possible to work on substructures of arrays. For example, a row of a matrix can be considered as a vector. In principle, in most cases a good compiler can avoid copying the subtructure into a work array. The Cray compiler cf90 3.4.0.0 is doing a good job from this point of view. However, other compilers frequently make unnecessary copies, requiring superfluous operations as well as additional memory.

5.18   Attaining peak speed

The speed of most realistic programs is limited by the slow memory access. However, a program that has no memory accesses and a perfect mix of additions and multiplications should run at peak speed. Such a program is listed below.

```
       subroutine sub_1(n,x1,x2,x3,x4)
       implicit real*8 (a-h,o-z)

       do 10,i=1,n
         y1=x1 + .500007500110d-05*x2 + .100001500023d-04*x3
         y2=x2 + .500007500110d-05*x1 + .100001500023d-04*x4
         y3=x3 + .100001500023d-04*x1 + .500007500110d-05*x4
         y4=x4 + .100001500023d-04*x2 + .500007500110d-05*x3

         x1=y1 + .500007500110d-05*y2 + .100001500023d-04*y3
         x2=y2 + .500007500110d-05*y1 + .100001500023d-04*y4
         x3=y3 + .100001500023d-04*y1 + .500007500110d-05*y4
         x4=y4 + .100001500023d-04*y2 + .500007500110d-05*y3
10     continue

       return
       end
```

This subroutine has no dependencies, a large degree of parallelism and no other features that might prevent it from running at peak speed. Nevertheless, we obtained peak performance from compiler-optimized code only on the IBM Power2 architecture where one loop iteration took exactly eight cycles. On machines without FMA instructions, software pipelining is much more difficult and the compiler-generated code runs at roughly half of the peak speed on the SGI R10000, Compaq/DEC EV6 and Cray T3E (compilers: MIPSpro_7.2.1, Compaq V5.2, Cray cf90 3.4.0.0). Software pipelining by hand, as shown in section A.3 of the appendix, was necessary to get good performance. In this case, we obtained peak speed on the R10000 and roughly 90% of the peak speed on the Compaq/DEC EV6 and T3E. This demonstrates, again, that even the best compilers have considerable difficulties in creating optimal code even in relatively simple cases. One reason is in the poor grouping of independent multiplications and additions by software pipelining, as necessary to keep the addition and multiplication units busy without stalls. Another problem that can prevent a program from reaching peak speed is unexpected pipeline stalls. On the IBM Power3 architecture, it was impossible to reach peak speed in the subroutine sub_1, even though it has a FMA instruction.

Chapter 6

Optimization of Memory Access

As has already been stressed several times in this book, memory access is the major bottleneck on machines with a memory hierarchy. Therefore, optimizing the memory access has the largest potential for performance improvements. While floating point optimization can speed up a program by a factor of 2 for in-cache data, memory access optimization can easily lead to performance improvements by a factor of 10 or more for out of cache data.

In this chapter we discuss issues pertinent to memory access optimization. For readability, many examples will present loop structures that were not unrolled or otherwise optimized according to the principles put forward in the previous chapter. When timings are presented, the floating point optimizations are done by hand or by invoking the compiler with appropriate options.

6.1 An illustration of the memory access times on RISC machines

Memory access times vary widely depending on how memory is accessed. This can be illustrated by a very simple copy routine "memory_test," listed in section A.4 of the appendix. We measure the time required for repeatedly copying elements separated by different strides (stride is the distance, measured in words, between two memory locations consecutively accessed by a code) in data sets of different sizes. The copying is repeated many times in order to gather meaningful statistics. After the first copy the data, or fractions of it, are in cache for the successive copy steps. The performance figures obtained from this program are shown in Table 6.1 for an IBM 590. The first column gives the number of cycles necessary to access the data with unit stride. For small data sets, the stride-1 performance is poor due to the significant overhead of the short loops. Going to larger data sets, we note a sudden increase in time once the two vectors to be copied are longer than

Table 6.1: *Average number of cycles per memory access for copying (one load and one store) data sets of different sizes accessed with different strides on an IBM 590 workstation. Data sizes and strides are shown as the log$_2$ of the actual sizes in doublewords. The boundaries of the cache and TLB are indicated by double horizontal lines.*

Data size \ Stride	0	1	2	3	4	5	6	7	8	9	10	11	12
4	1.822												
5	1.338	5.4											
6	1.021	3.3	5.3										
7	.850	1.7	3.2	5.3									
8	.772	1.6	2.1	3.3	5.3								
9	.729	1.3	1.6	2.1	3.3	5.2							
10	.713	1.1	1.3	1.6	2.2	3.3	5.1						
11	.696	1.1	1.2	1.3	1.6	2.1	3.3	5.3					
12	.691	1.0	1.1	1.3	1.6	1.6	2.1	3.3	5.2				
13	.688	1.0	1.0	1.1	1.3	1.3	1.6	2.2	3.3	5.2			
14	.688	1.0	1.1	1.1	1.2	1.4	1.3	1.6	2.1	3.3	5.2		
15	1.829	3.7	7.7	15.2	29.3	52.5	52.6	52.9	53.3	54.7	53.9	5.2	
16	1.836	3.7	7.8	15.1	29.3	52.3	52.3	52.6	52.6	53.2	53.1	53.5	37.4
17	1.837	3.7	7.8	15.2	29.2	52.6	52.4	52.3	52.7	52.9	52.7	52.9	53.4
18	1.845	3.7	8.0	15.3	31.0	53.6	53.1	52.9	52.7	52.9	53.0	53.7	54.8
19	1.855	3.7	8.0	15.4	29.6	53.1	53.1	53.0	53.3	53.3	53.1	53.6	53.5
20	1.856	3.7	8.0	15.4	29.8	53.1	53.3	53.4	53.4	53.9	53.8	54.1	54.1

2^{14} double precision (8 byte) words. The reason is that the IBM 590 machine has an L1 cache that can hold $2^{15} = 32768$ double precision words. The same drop in performance can be seen in the other columns that correspond to larger strides. A second, much smaller, increase in the stride-1 access time is noticeable when the data set becomes larger than 2^{17} words. This increase is due to the TLB, which has a capacity of 2^{18} on the IBM 590 workstation. The reason why the jump at the TLB boundary is smaller than at the L1 cache boundary is the following. A page is much larger than a cache line. The cost of a cache and TLB miss, on the other hand, are of the same order of magnitude. In stride-1 data access the cost of a TLB miss is distributed among the many elements of a page, whereas the cost of a cache miss is only distributed among the few elements of a cache line.

Let us look next at the performance as a function of the stride for out of cache data sizes, presented in the rows in the lower part of the table. This performance decreases continuously and then saturates for strides larger than or equal to 32. The asymptotic value, 27 to 28 cycles for a memory copy, is quite high. This reveals that the cache line size is 32 doublewords for this machine and that the latency for the transfer of this cache line from memory to cache is between 27 and 28 cycles. Loading all of the 32 words takes slightly longer than just loading every 32nd element, namely, 32 cycles.

Exercise: Show that the measurements of Table 6.1 are consistent with the numbers presented in Figure 2.2 for the same machine.

This discussion clearly shows that best performance is obtained when data exhibits temporal locality. In this case, the data fits in cache and it is reused many times in the repeated copy operations. On an IBM 590, the average cost for a load/store in this case is only .3 cycles. The second best case is when spatial data locality is present. This is essentially the stride-1 case, where all the array elements that are loaded into cache are used at least once. The cost of a cache miss is distributed over all the entries of one cache line. On the IBM 590, the cost of a load/store is close to one cycle in this case.

In many scientific calculations the data sets are too large to fit in cache and temporal data locality cannot be obtained by restructuring the code. In this case, we should strive to achieve spatial locality of data.

A simple example for a calculation of this type is the orthogonalization of a vector y to a vector x of unit length. In the first step, we calculate the scalar product s between the two vectors, $s = \sum_i x(i) * y(i)$. This computation requires loads of all the vector elements. In the second step, a DAXPY calculation is performed, $y(i) = y(i) - s * x(i)$, where, again, all the array elements need to be loaded. Obviously, it is not possible to reformulate this calculation in such a way that the two steps are carried on simultaneously on chunks of the two vectors and then synthesize the result at the end. If the vectors are large enough so that they don't completely fit in cache, then the temporal locality is lost, but the two steps exhibit spatial data locality.

6.2   Performance of various computers for unit and large stride data access

Because of the importance of spatial data locality in scientific computations, it is interesting to see how well different RISC processors, as well as vector processors, perform in this regime, in the absence of temporal data locality. The results of such a test are shown in Figure 6.1. The data were obtained in the same way as the one in Table 6.1, but only the first column was used, after being converted from cycles/copy to units of megacopies/second (hereafter abbreviated Mcopies/sec).

Several comments are in order here. First, the drastically different behavior of a vector machine, as represented by the Cray C90, compared to all the RISC workstations is striking. Whereas for the RISC workstations the performance for large data sets becomes quite poor, it does not decay at all on the vector machine. This is due to the fact that the vector machine does not have a cache, but can very rapidly load data sets from memory directly into the vector registers. On the other hand, the performance of the vector machine is quite poor for short loop lengths, where the number of data accessed is much smaller than the size of the vector registers. The large latency associated with the loading of a vector register cannot be distributed among many data items in this case. We have chosen a somewhat outdated vector machine, the Cray C90, for this comparison to avoid obtaining data that are out of scale with respect to the RISC data. On a Cray T90, the asymptotic bandwidth is much larger than on a C90, namely, 720 Mcopies/sec.

A second interesting observation is that the memory bandwidth is not correlated at all with the CPU cycle time. The Cray T3E, the DEC EV5 and the Compaq/DEC EV6 all have clock speeds in the range of 400 to 500 MHz. As a matter of fact, the Cray T3E processor is identical to the DEC EV5. Nevertheless, the memory bandwidth of the Cray T3E is significantly better than the one of the EV5. This is due to the fact that Cray utilizes stream buffers to improve the memory bandwidth. Stream buffers do hardware prefetching, as will be discussed in more detail in section 6.11. The improvement of the EV6 over its predecessor EV5 is due to a doubling of the number of load/store units, i.e., to an increased on-chip parallelism, as well as to a faster bus.

On the IBM, newer isn't necessarily better as far as memory bandwidth goes. The new Power3 260 processor has a lower bandwidth than its Power2 397 predecessor. For in-cache data, the reason for the inferior performance is that the new Power3 processor no longer has a load instruction that can load two adjacent doublewords per cycle. For out of cache data, the lower performance is partly due to the fact that our test loop does not activate the stream buffers (see section 6.11).

Even though several of the computers (Compaq Alpha, Cray T3E, IBM 260) whose bandwidth is plotted in Figure 6.1 have more than one cache level, the L1 cache is not visible in most of these plots. The reason is that the L1 cache is so small that it influences data locality only for very small data sets and therefore for very small loop lengths. In this situation, loop overheads become a leading performance degradation factor. The peak performance is always reached for data sets that fill

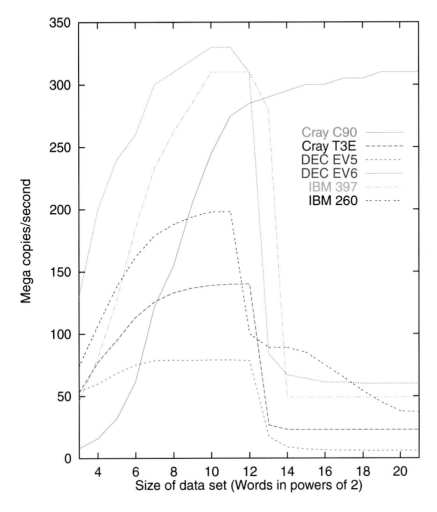

Figure 6.1: *The memory bandwidth in megacopy operations per second for different data sizes (given in powers of 2) on different computers.*

the higher cache levels. The only exception is the IBM 260, where both cache levels are fairly large and thus visible on the plot.

We have to point out that by using different compiler flags or by using BLAS instead of our own copy routine, different results from those shown in Figure 6.1 can be obtained. From Table 2.1, we could expect a performance close to 500 Mcopies/sec for small data sets on the EV6 clocked at 500 MHz. With low optimization ($-$O2), we get close to this number, however, the asymptotic value is reduced by 50%. At higher optimization levels the compiler includes additional prefetch instructions (see section 6.11) that boost the asymptotic out of cache performance but lower the in-cache performance. Vector architectures do not perform

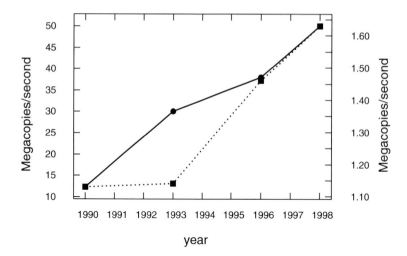

Figure 6.2: *The performance (in Mcopies/sec) for various IBM Power1 and Power2 workstations for local stride 1 (left y-axis, solid line) and nonlocal stride 64 (right y-axis, dashed line) data access. While the performance for spatial data locality has strongly increased over the time period considered, it has increased very little for non-local copying.*

well on unrolled loops. Indeed, the performance on the C90 was somewhat lower on our unrolled loop than that of the simplest loop, 310 instead of 430 Mcopies/sec.

Extensive memory bandwidth data for the most common computers can be found at http://www.cs.virginia.edu/stream/.

Let us next examine the worst-case scenario, that of nonlocal data access. In this context it is particularly interesting to look at historical data. For this perspective, we have chosen the IBM RS/6000 computer line since it is characterized by a relatively high memory bandwidth. Even for this class of machines the performance in this regime is quite low, as shown in Figure 6.2. Even more surprisingly, the performance for nonlocal data access has increased very little over the past 10 years. This has to be compared with the huge increase in CPU floating point performance shown in Figure 1.1. This is an illustration of the "memory wall effect" that many researchers refer to in the literature. The cost of memory access becomes higher and higher in terms of CPU cycles as the speed of the CPU increases. For nonlocal data access, the superiority of vector processors is even more striking than for stride-1 data access. Traditional vector machines retain their stride-1 performance, over 300 Mcopies/sec on the Cray C90. Even the new low-cost, cache-based vector systems from Cray, such as the SV1, still achieve 150 Mcopies/sec. This is due to a very large number of memory banks and to a cache line size of a single word.

Given this slow increase in performance for nonlocal data access, the question arises as to why the performance for the case of spatial data locality kept up with the increase in CPU speed, as shown in Figure 1.1. The main reason is in the increase of the cache line size. In this way, the cache miss penalty is distributed over more loads/stores for local data access, resulting in a nearly constant penalty per load/store.

For traditional vector machines, the bandwidth is independent of the stride as long as the stride is not a multiple of a power of 2. The advantages of such machines over RISC machines for nonlocal data access are significant.

Some RISC machines have interleaved caches. The principles are exactly the same as in the case of vector computers whose memory is interleaved (section 2.9). As a consequence, the data access speed depends on the stride even for in-cache data. As in the case of vector machines, strides of 2 or a multiple of a power of 2 should be avoided.

6.3   Loop reordering for optimal data locality

The following code sequences differ in their loop ordering only:

```
      dimension a(n,n),b(n,n)              dimension a(n,n),b(n,n)
C     LOOP A                        C      LOOP B
      do 10,i=1,n                          do 20,j=1,n
      do 10,j=1,n                          do 20,i=1,n
10    a(i,j)=b(i,j)                 20     a(i,j)=b(i,j)
```

Let us discuss the memory access patterns of these two loops for the case of small and of big matrices. To simplify the analysis we assume that the size of the cache is very small, 128 double precision numbers only. In this case, a matrix is small when n is less than eight words, and therefore both a and b fit in cache. The length of a cache line is assumed to be eight doublewords. According to the Fortran convention, the physical ordering of matrix elements in memory is the following:

```
a(1,1),a(2,1),a(3,1),  ... ,a(n,1) , a(1,2),a(2,2), a(3,2), ... ,a(n,2), .......
```

We refer to this access pattern as "column major order." In C, the storage convention is just the opposite, "row major order," meaning that the last index is "running fastest." Therefore, the physical indexing of our small ($n = 8$) and big ($n = 16$) matrices is the following, in Fortran:

```
1    9   17   25   33   41   49   57
2   10   18   26   34   42   50   58
3   11   19   27   35   43   51   59
4   12   20   28   36   44   52   60
5   13   21   29   37   45   53   61
6   14   22   30   38   46   54   62
7   15   23   31   39   47   55   63
8   16   24   32   40   48   56   64
```

1	17	33	49	65	81	97	113	129	145	161	177	193	209	225	241
2	18	34	50	66	82	98	114	130	146	162	178	194	210	226	242
3	19	35	51	67	83	99	115	131	147	163	179	195	211	227	243
4	20	36	52	68	84	100	116	132	148	164	180	196	212	228	244
5	21	37	53	69	85	101	117	133	149	165	181	197	213	229	245
6	22	38	54	70	86	102	118	134	150	166	182	198	214	230	246
7	23	39	55	71	87	103	119	135	151	167	183	199	215	231	247
8	24	40	56	72	88	104	120	136	152	168	184	200	216	232	248
9	25	41	57	73	89	105	121	137	153	169	185	201	217	233	249
10	26	42	58	74	90	106	122	138	154	170	186	202	218	234	250
11	27	43	59	75	91	107	123	139	155	171	187	203	219	235	251
12	28	44	60	76	92	108	124	140	156	172	188	204	220	236	252
13	29	45	61	77	93	109	125	141	157	173	189	205	221	237	253
14	30	46	62	78	94	110	126	142	158	174	190	206	222	238	254
15	31	47	63	79	95	111	127	143	159	175	191	207	223	239	255
16	32	48	64	80	96	112	128	144	160	176	192	208	224	240	256

In the following discussion we assume that the first matrix elements of both a and b are aligned on a cache line boundary; i.e., the first element of each matrix is also the first element of a cache line. We also assume that all the data are out of cache at the beginning of the calculation.

We distinguish the following cases:

- Loop A, small matrices: In this case the matrix elements will be accessed in the following order:

  ```
  x(1,1),x(1,2),x(1,3), .. ,x(1,8) , x(2,1),x(2,2),x(2,3), .. , x(2,8), .....
  ```

  where x denotes either a or b. However, this is not the physical order in memory. The elements $x(1,i)$ and $x(1,i+1)$ are actually eight doublewords apart, and thus a cache miss will occur on the first eight loads of both a and b, as we access the physical memory locations 1, 9, 17, 25, 33, 41, 49 and 57. Since the cache can house all of the $2 \times 8^2 = 128$ doublewords that were brought in during the first eight iterations of the double loop, all subsequent memory references will be cache hits. No other cache misses will occur in all of the remaining loop iterations. The load of all the 2×8^2 elements involved 2×8 cache misses, i.e., one cache miss for every 8 words.

- Loop A, big matrices: The memory access pattern will be the same as above; i.e., consecutive memory references are not adjacent. In this case they are 16 doublewords apart. After the first 16 iterations of the loop (each of which caused a cache miss) we will have loaded 2×16 cache lines, i.e., $2 \times 16 \times 8 = 128$ doublewords. The cache will be full. All of the subsequent cache lines loaded will need to overwrite the existing ones. The old cache lines will be flushed out of cache and stored back in the main memory. The cache line holding elements 129 to 136 will replace the cache line holding elements 1 to 8, the cache line holding elements 145 to 152 will replace the cache line holding elements 17 to 24, and so on. In the second iteration of the outer loop, the array element $x(2, 1)$, which was loaded in cache along with $x(1, 1)$, will no longer be available, as its cache line was replaced. This implies that the number of cache misses is now 2×16^2, i.e., one cache miss for every word accessed.

- Loop B: In this case we access the matrix elements exactly in the order in which they are stored in memory. We will then have one cache miss for every 8 doublewords for both small and large matrices. All the data brought in cache by the cache misses will be reused by the subsequent inner loop iterations.

We see that, for large matrices, the loop structure A results in a significant performance loss. For a realistically scaled-up example, the performance degrades by roughly a factor of 30 on an IBM 590 when using loop A instead of loop B. Loop B gives the best data locality and is always to be preferred, even though in the case of small matrices the performance is the same for both orderings. The above conclusion remains valid in the more stringent, but realistic case, where the matrices are not aligned on a cache line boundary. The hardware performance monitor output that we have listed in section 4.5 for both loop structures confirms our reasoning. For out of cache data, the number of cache misses (marked by an arrow) is enormous.

This example was chosen for didactic reasons only. In practice, for array copying, using the BLAS DCOPY routine is recommended. By using the calling sequence

```
call DCOPY(n*n,b,1,a,1)
```

the matrices a and b are considered as one-dimensional vectors of length n^2 and the copying is done optimally from a data locality standpoint. At high optimization levels good performance can be obtained without BLAS if the compiler collapses the two loops into a single one.

Exercise: Find out what constitutes a "big" and a "small" matrix for your workstation and compare the timings for loops A and B in the case of big matrices.

6.4 Loop fusion to reduce unnecessary memory references

Let us look at the following section of a molecular dynamics code, performing the update of the position and velocity of n particles.

```
c UPDATE VELOCITIES
      do 10 i=1,n
      do 10 j=1,3
        at = fxyz(j,i)
        vxyz(j,i)= vxyz(j,i) + (.5d0*dt/rmass) * (at + gxyz(j,i))
        gxyz(j,i) = at
10    continue
c UPDATE POSITIONS
      do 20 i=1,n
      do 20 j=1,3
        rxyz(j,i)=rxyz(j,i)+ dt*vxyz(j,i) + (.5d0*dt*dt/rmass)*fxyz(j,i)
20    continue
```

The velocities $vxyz(j,i)$ and the forces $fxyz(j,i)$, stored in the velocity update section of the code, need to be reloaded in the position update loop. The two superfluous reloads can be avoided if the loops are fused into a single one as shown below. The performance gain will be particularly large for big data sets when the elements are flushed out of cache before being reloaded. The compiler will load $vxyz(j,i)$ and $fxyz(j,i)$ once only, storing the array elements in registers between their two uses within the same loop iteration.

```
      c UPDATE POSITIONS AND VELOCITIES
      do 10 i=1,n
      do 10 j=1,3
        at = fxyz(j,i)
        vxyz(j,i)= vxyz(j,i) + (.5d0*dt/rmass) * (at + gxyz(j,i))
        gxyz(j,i) = at
        rxyz(j,i)=rxyz(j,i)+ dt*vxyz(j,i) + (.5d0*dt*dt/rmass)*fxyz(j,i)
10      continue
```

Most compilers do loop fusion at the highest optimization level.

6.5 Data locality and the conceptual layout of a program

In order to achieve optimal data locality, the data structures in a program need to be designed in such a way that quantities that are used in the same context are physically close in memory. Choosing optimal data structures is a very important point and should be done when starting the development of a program, as changing them for an existing program can be cumbersome. Let us look at the following two versions of the main loop in a molecular dynamics code. The forces are summed up for all particles separated by a distance smaller than the interaction range of the potential "cutoff."

```
DATA STRUCTURE A
      dimension rx(n),ry(n),rz(n),fx(n),fy(n),fz(n)

c loop over all particle pairs
      do 100,i=1,n
      do 100,j=1,i-1
        dist2=(rx(i)-rx(j))**2 + (ry(i)-ry(j))**2 +(rz(i)-rz(j))**2
        if (dist2.le.cutoff2) then
c calculate interaction
            dfx= ......
            dfy= ......
            dfz= ......
c accumulate force
            fx(j)=fx(j)+dfx
            fy(j)=fy(j)+dfy
            fz(j)=fz(j)+dfz
            fx(i)=fx(i)-dfx
            fy(i)=fy(i)-dfy
            fz(i)=fz(i)-dfz
        endif
100     continue
```

```
DATA STRUCTURE B
        dimension r(3,n),f(3,n)

c loop over all particle pairs
        do 100,i=1,n
        do 100,j=1,i-1
          dist2=(r(1,i)-r(1,j))**2 + (r(2,i)-r(2,j))**2 +(r(3,i)-r(3,j))**2
          if (dist2.le.cutoff2) then
c calculate interaction
              dfx= ......
              dfy= ......
              dfz= ......
c accumulate force
              f(1,j)=f(1,j)+dfx
              f(2,j)=f(2,j)+dfy
              f(3,j)=f(3,j)+dfz
              f(1,i)=f(1,i)-dfx
              f(2,i)=f(2,i)-dfy
              f(3,i)=f(3,i)-dfz
          endif
100     continue
```

The memory access patterns of the array elements $fx(j)$, $fy(j)$ and $fz(j)$ will be more or less random. We cannot expect that if particle j is close to particle i, then particle $j+1$ will also be close to particle i. This means that memory references for the $(j+1)$th force component, brought into cache by accessing the j component, will most likely be overwritten in cache before used in a later accumulation step (we assume here that the cache is not big enough to hold all the data). Therefore, we essentially have one cache miss for every force component reference indexed by j. For the three existing force components in data structure A, three cache misses occur. For data structure B, we can load all of the three components indexed by j under one cache miss since they are adjacent in memory. The data structure B is therefore more efficient.

6.6   Cache thrashing

As explained in section 2.4, cache thrashing occurs if the effective size of the cache is much smaller than its physical size because of the constraints of the mapping rules. In this section we analyze cases where cache thrashing can occur in codes. Let us look at the following program.

```
        program cache_thrash
        implicit real*8 (a-h,o-z)
c array x without buffer
        parameter(nx=2**13,nbuf=0)
c array x with buffer
C       parameter(nx=2**13,nbuf=81)
```

```
      dimension x(nx+nbuf,6)

      nl=2**10
      call sub(nl,x(1,1),x(1,2),x(1,3),x(1,4),x(1,5),x(1,6))
      end



      subroutine sub(n,x1,x2,x3,x4,y1,y2)
      implicit real*8 (a-h,o-z)
      dimension x1(n),x2(n),x3(n),x4(n),y1(n),y2(n)

      do 15,i=1,n-1,2
        y1(i+0)=x1(i+0)+x2(i+0)
        y1(i+1)=x1(i+1)+x2(i+1)
        y2(i+0)=x3(i+0)+x4(i+0)
        y2(i+1)=x3(i+1)+x4(i+1)
15    continue

      return
      end
```

On an IBM 590, with $nbuf$=0 we get a performance of just 3.5 Mflops, whereas 67 Mflops is achieved with $nbuf$=81 or any other reasonable nonzero value. Note that we did not modify the subroutine that is doing the numerical work at all. The reason for the extremely poor performance, in the first case, is that all six memory references are mapped to the same four slots in cache (Figure 2.3). So, even though all the data of size $6 \times 2^{10} = 6144$ words that are accessed in the subroutine could easily fit in cache, the effective cache size in this case is only four cache lines ($4 \times 32 = 128$ doublewords), which is not enough to hold all of the six cache lines. This example is of course contrived. In most applications the starting elements of these six arrays will not be separated by a high power of 2. However, there are many algorithms, most notably fast Fourier transforms, fast multipole methods, multigrid methods and wavelet transforms, where the leading dimensions are typically high powers of 2. Padding the arrays will fix the performance problem in these cases. It is clear that the likelihood of running into cache thrashing is higher for directly mapped caches than for set associative ones.

On a computer with several cache levels, cache thrashing can occur for each level as well as for the TLB. In dealing with this, we recommend the conservative assumption that all memory levels behave like inclusive caches. This means that strides (usually leading dimensions) need to be adjusted in such a way that conflict cache misses are avoided for all cache levels.

Even in the absence of arrays with pathological cache behavior, there will seldom be perfect mapping. Good usage of the cache size is particularly difficult in the case of directly mapped caches. In this case, in order to increase the effective cache size, the arrays may have to be aligned by hand in memory. This can be done by copying them in a work array and choosing the starting positions of the subarrays in the work array in an optimal way. An alternative is to align them in a common block. The first method has the advantage that the starting positions can be chosen dynamically. For the program cache_thrash this first solution can be implemented as follows:

```
implicit real*8 (a-h,o-z)
parameter(nn=1024,nx=2**15)
dimension w(nn*6),x(nx,6),ist(6)

nl=....
x=.....


iist=1
do j=1,6
  ist(j)=iist
  do i=1,nl
    w(iist)=x(i,j)
    iist=iist+1
  enddo
enddo

call sub(nl,w(ist(1)),w(ist(2)),w(ist(3)),
&           w(ist(4)),w(ist(5)),w(ist(6)))
end
```

6.7 Experimental determination of cache and TLB parameters

Relevant parameters of the memory hierarchy, such as the total cache size, the cache associativity, the length of a cache line, the total TLB size, its associativity and the page size, are often hidden in vendor documentation in a wealth of other information useful to a system architect but seldom to a programmer. An experimental determination of these parameters is then necessary. We have already demonstrated in section 6.1 how to extract the cache size, TLB size and cache line size from the memory access times. Below, we have listed a cleverly designed test program that can be used to determine the cache associativity by taking advantage of the cache thrashing effect. The generalization of the code fragment shown below for higher values of *iassoc* should be obvious. All of the loops have been unrolled by hand to exhibit enough parallelism and to reduce loop overheads.

```
subroutine assoc_thrash(m,n1,n2,nit,iassoc,izero,a)
implicit real*8 (a-h,o-z)
dimension a(n1,n2)

if (iassoc.eq.1) then

  do 1,i=1,nit
  tt=i
  do 1,j=1,m-7,8
    a(j+0,1)=tt
    a(j+1,1)=tt
    a(j+2,1)=tt
    a(j+3,1)=tt
    a(j+4,1)=tt
    a(j+5,1)=tt
```

```
            a(j+6,1)=tt
            a(j+7,1)=tt
1           continue

        else if (iassoc.eq.2) then

          do 10,i=1,nit
          tt=i
          do 10,j=1,m-3,4
            a(j+0,1)=tt
            a(j+0,2)=tt
            a(j+1,1)=tt
            a(j+1,2)=tt
            a(j+2,1)=tt
            a(j+2,2)=tt
            a(j+3,1)=tt
            a(j+3,2)=tt
10          continue

        else if (iassoc.eq.3) then

          .............
```

This subroutine accesses the first m elements of *iassoc* columns of the matrix a that have a leading dimension $n1$. For better timing statistics, the inner loop is repeated *nit* times. The value of m has to be smaller than $n1$, but large enough for the loop overheads to be negligible. Let us now assume that the cache has m_{as} associativity classes and a total size of $m_{as} * ncache\_size$. Whenever the leading dimension $n1$ is equal to *ncache_size*, all of the *iassoc* elements in one row are mapped to the same m_{as} slots in cache. As a result, the effective capacity of the cache is greatly reduced. Consequently, if we access more than m_{as} elements, the access time will sharply increase. The same effect will be observed for higher cache levels and for the TLB. The timing output of the subroutine "assoc_thrash" is shown in Table 6.2 for an IBM 590 with one cache level and a TLB.

Table 6.2 clearly shows that cache thrashing occurs as soon as one tries to fit in the cache more than four columns of the matrix a, each longer than 8192. Consequently the cache is four-way associative and has a total capacity of 4×8192 doublewords. Based on similar type of observations, it turns out that the TLB is two-way associative with a total capacity of 2×131072 doublewords. Estimates for the penalties due to cache and TLB misses can also deduced from Table 6.2. On this architecture, a cache miss costs at least 35 cycles and a TLB miss at least 3 cycles. Extracting exact numbers from such measurements is difficult. The effective cache miss cost, when more than one miss is outstanding, is not a simple sum of the cost of each miss. In the same way, there are interference effects for simultaneous cache and TLB misses. Another useful parameter is the page size. Its experimental determination is difficult. Fortunately many machines have a "pagesize" command that will return this parameter.

Table 6.2: *Data access times measured by the subroutine "assoc_thrash" on an IBM 590. The first column shows the $\log_2$ of the size of the leading dimension in doublewords. The second column shows the size of the leading dimension in doublewords. The other columns give the access times for iassoc ranging from one to eight.*

7	128	.8	.8	.8	.8	.8	.8	.8	.8
8	256	.8	.9	.8	.8	.8	.8	.8	.8
9	512	.8	.9	.8	.8	.8	.8	.8	.8
10	1024	.8	.9	.8	.8	.8	.8	.8	.8
11	2048	.8	.8	.8	.9	.8	.8	.8	.8
12	4096	.9	.7	.8	.8	.8	.8	.8	.8
13	8192	.8	.9	.8	.8	36.5	35.8	35.8	35.8
14	16384	.8	.9	.8	.8	36.5	35.8	35.8	35.8
15	32768	.8	.9	.8	.8	36.7	35.8	35.6	35.7
16	65536	.9	.8	.8	.9	37.4	37.8	37.8	37.8
17	131072	.9	.8	3.3	6.0	37.3	37.4	37.8	37.8
18	262144	.8	.9	3.3	6.2	37.8	37.8	37.8	37.5

6.8 Finding optimal strides

In this section we are analyzing data access patterns with nonunit stride. Such a pattern can arise if several rows of a matrix are accessed in Fortran, given Fortran's column major access convention. Even if the entire matrix does not fit in cache, it is usually possible to hold a sufficiently large number of rows in cache by choosing appropriate strides. Thus, data locality can be obtained. Strides can be adjusted by making the leading dimension of a matrix larger than its logical dimension, i.e., by padding the matrix with a few rows whose numerical values do not matter.

The easiest way to find optimal strides is by simulation. By knowing the mapping rule, we can predict the location in cache where a cache line can be accommodated. By keeping track of the cache line slots already occupied we can determine whether, given the effective cache capacity, the cache is full or not. A simulation program of this type is listed below. It returns the number of cache lines *lot* that fit in cache for a fixed stride *nd*, given the cache size "ncache_size" and the cache line size "ncache_line."

```
      subroutine cache_par(ncache_line,ncache_size,nd,lot)
      implicit real*8 (a-h,o-z)
      logical lch
      parameter(mlx=1024)
      dimension lch(0:mlx-1)
c INPUT:
c     ncache_line: size of cache line in doublewords
c     massoc: number of associativity classes for the cache
c     ncache_size: size of one associativity class of the cache
c              (total cache size is massoc*ncache_size)
c     nd: stride (frequently = leading dimension of a matrix)
c OUTPUT:
c     lot: maximum number of items that fit into cache (=blocking size)
```

```
        ml=ncache_size/ncache_line
        if (ml.gt.mlx) stop 'enlarge mlx'


c all cache lines are empty
        do i=0,ml-1
        lch(i)=.true.
        enddo


c set cache line number to an impossible value
        iold=-1
c initialize memory address (jnd=j*nd)
        jnd=0
c initialize counter for number of items that fit into cache
        j=0


100     continue
c address jnd is im-th word in cache
        im=mod(jnd,ncache_size)
c imth word is in ith cache line
        i=im/ncache_line


c if consecutive data are on the same cache line skip the if tests
        if (nd.le.ncache_line .and. i.eq.iold) goto 150


c check if cache line is already occupied
          if (lch(i)) then
c    it not occupy it
             lch(i)=.false.
          else
c else effective cache size reached
             lot=j
             goto 222
          endif


150     continue
c save old cache line number
        iold=i
c update counter for number of items that fit into cache
        j=j+1
c the cache cannot hold more than ncache_size entries
        if (j.gt.ncache_size) stop 'error cache_par'
c update memory address (jnd=j*nd)
        jnd=jnd+nd


        goto 100


222     continue


        return
        end
```

Table 6.3: *The first line gives the original strides that are powers of 2, the second line the adjusted strides that were slightly increased to avoid cache thrashing on an IBM 590 workstation.*

Orig. stride	1	2	4	8	16	32	64	128	256	512	1024	2048	4096	8192
Adj. stride	1	2	4	8	16	32	68	136	257	514	1028	2056	4112	8224

In order to get the optimal stride, the recipe is to run "cache_par" for increasingly large values of nd until an nd is obtained that gives the full physical cache size. The details can be looked up in section A.4 of the appendix, where the full program "memory_test" is listed. The adjusted strides obtained in this way are shown in Table 6.3.

With these modified strides, the program memory_test gives the memory access times shown in Table 6.4.

The most striking difference, comparing the results in Table 6.4 with those in Table 6.1, is that the access times improve for large strides, indicating that the referenced elements of the data set fit in cache. For instance, we can now accommodate all the elements of the two 2^{17}-word vectors that are stride 2^8 apart in the cache. Indeed, that should be possible. In this case we access 2^9 elements of each vector. Since an entire cache line of length 32 is loaded, we actually load 2^{14} elements. Since the total cache size is 2^{15}, all the data should fit in. The reason why they did not fit in for the measurements presented in Table 6.1 is that, in that case, the strides were not adjusted and consequently cache thrashing occurred.

Even though we adjusted the stride explicitly only in such a way as to avoid cache thrashing, TLB thrashing was, by chance, eliminated too. This can be seen from the fact that we get rather short access times for data sets that do not fit in the TLB.

6.9   Square blocking

Square blocking (or tiling) is a strategy for obtaining spatial data locality in loops where it is not possible to have small strides for all referenced arrays. One simple example is a matrix transposition, performed by the program below.

```
        subroutine rot(n,a,b)
        implicit real*8 (a-h,o-z)
        dimension a(n,n),b(n,n)

        do 100,i=1,n
        do 100,j=1,n
          b(j,i)=a(i,j)
100     continue

        return
        end
```

Table 6.4: *Same as Table 6.1, but with the adjusted strides of Table 6.3.*

Data size	0	1	2	3	4	5	6	7	8	9	10	11	12
4	1.564												
5	1.176	4.6											
6	.990	2.8	4.6										
7	.860	2.0	2.8	4.5									
8	.798	1.5	2.0	2.9	4.6								
9	.774	1.2	1.4	2.0	2.8	4.6							
10	.745	1.1	1.2	1.5	2.0	2.8	4.9						
11	.757	1.1	1.1	1.2	1.5	2.0	2.9	4.9					
12	.751	1.0	1.1	1.1	1.2	1.5	1.9	3.0	4.6				
13	.756	1.0	1.0	1.0	1.0	1.1	1.4	1.9	2.8	4.5			
14	.764	1.0	1.1	1.1	1.2	1.4	1.3	1.5	2.0	2.9	4.6		
15	1.824	3.6	7.5	16.5	30.8	55.0	1.5	1.4	1.6	2.2	3.5	4.6	
16	1.837	3.7	7.3	16.4	30.7	55.1	56.6	2.1	1.3	1.6	2.3	2.9	4.6
17	1.845	3.7	7.4	16.5	30.9	54.8	57.0	57.7	1.3	1.3	1.6	2.0	2.8
18	1.860	3.7	7.4	16.4	31.3	55.6	58.0	60.4	60.3	29.6	1.3	1.5	2.0
19	1.862	3.7	7.4	16.8	31.2	55.8	58.2	60.9	61.5	66.3	55.8	1.3	1.6
20	1.867	3.7	7.3	16.7	31.2	55.6	58.1	60.8	61.5	66.5	78.1	83.7	1.3
	S	S	T	T	T	R	R	I	D	D	D	E	E

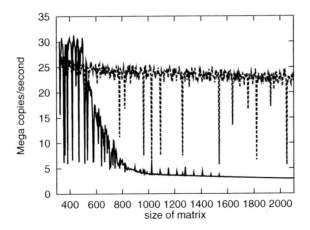

Figure 6.3: *Performance of a matrix transposition with (dashed line) and without (solid line) blocking. In the absence of blocking the performance decreases dramatically for large matrix sizes. The performance of the blocked version stays fairly constant with the exception of certain matrix sizes where cache thrashing occurs.*

Obviously, it is not possible to have unit stride access for the elements of the arrays a and b at the same time. For large data sets that do not fit in cache, the performance degradation is significant, as shown in Figure 6.3.

The fact that reasonable performance is achieved for small data sets suggests the solution for large data sets. Instead of transposing the matrix in one big chunk, we subdivide it into smaller submatrices and we transpose each of the smaller arrays. This divide-and-conquer strategy is called blocking and is shown schematically in Figure 6.4. The submatrices are indicated by different hashing patterns.

The Fortran implementation of the blocked version is the following:

```
      subroutine rotb(n,a,b,lot)
      implicit real*8 (a-h,o-z)
      dimension a(n,n),b(n,n)

c loop over blocks
      do 100,ii=1,n,lot
      do 100,jj=1,n,lot
c loop over elements in each block
      do 100,i=ii,min(n,ii+(lot-1))
      do 100,j=jj,min(n,jj+(lot-1))
        b(j,i)=a(i,j)
100      continue

      return
      end
```

The blocking parameter *lot* depends on the cache size. If the full physical cache were available, then *lot* would be chosen such that $2 \times lot^2 =$ the cache size. Because of the mapping rules previously discussed, the effective cache size is smaller than the physical cache size and we have to choose a smaller value of *lot*. The exact value could be determined by using subroutine "cache_par." Simply taking the effective

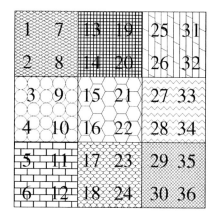

Figure 6.4: *Schematic representation of a blocked matrix transposition. The matrices are first subdivided into submatrices (in this case of size 2 by 2) denoted by differently hashed backgrounds, and then each pair of submatrices is transposed.*

cache size as equal to half the physical cache size works reasonably well for most matrix sizes, but cache thrashing occurs for some values, as shown in Figure 6.3.

An interesting question is whether it is necessary to square block with respect to several levels of the memory hierarchy, such as for the L1 cache, L2 cache and the TLB. According to our experience that is usually not necessary. L1 caches are usually small and blocking for them will lead to poorly performing short loops. Blocking for the TLB is necessary only for very large data sets. In addition, the number of TLB misses is, in general, negligible compared to the number of cache misses. In the case of a three-level memory hierarchy, it is only necessary to block for the L2 cache. The new IBM Power3 architecture, with large L1 and L2 caches, might be an exception to this rule.

Blocking is error prone and the code is likely to become less legible. Most compilers do square blocking when invoked with certain options. We verified that the IBM and SGI compilers generate optimal blocking, if invoked appropriately, in this easy example. For more complicated loops, such as those we will present in section 9.4, compilers are unlikely to do a satisfactory blocking job.

6.10   Line blocking

Square blocking is based on a static picture. A big matrix is subdivided into smaller rectangular matrices, on which we work sequentially. Square blocking causes a doubling of the number of loops. Line blocking, also called row- or column-oriented blocking, is based on the understanding of the dynamics of the data flow through the cache. Whereas in simple blocking rectangular (or square) blocks are utilized whose size is related to the size of the cache, irregular domains (Figure 6.7) can be used in line blocking, as will be explained in the following. The advantage is that fewer loops are needed and, in general, the innermost loops are longer.

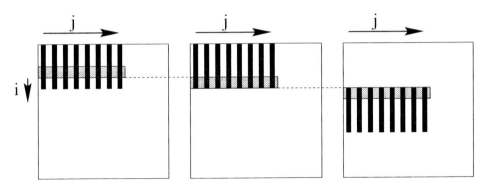

Figure 6.5: *Areas of the matrix a that are used during three successive iterations of the i-loop in the subroutine "rots." The leading dimension n of a is taken to be 12, the blocking parameter lot is 8. A cache line holds four doublewords. The elements accessed for fixed values of i are denoted by the hashed horizontal bars. The cache lines to which these elements belong are indicated by black vertical bars. Since "rots" is written in Fortran, the matrix is stored in column major order.*

To derive line blocking let us start with the blocked version of the matrix transposition subroutine *rotb*. Evidently, the algorithm is independent of the order in which we visit the different blocks. Hence, we can switch the order of the ii and jj loops. In addition, we can also merge the ii and i loops to obtain

```
      subroutine rots(n,a,b,lot)
      implicit real*8 (a-h,o-z)
      dimension a(n,n),b(n,n)

      do 100,jj=1,n,lot
      do 100,i=1,n
      do 100,j=jj,min(n,jj+(lot-1))
        b(j,i)=a(i,j)
100   continue

      return
      end
```

Let us first consider the simplest, but unlikely, case where the leading dimension n is a multiple of the cache line length. For the moment we will only concentrate on the data access pattern for the array a, since the array b has the best spatial data locality due to its stride-1 access. The array elements of a needed at different stages of transposition, as well as their location in cache, are shown in Figure 6.5.

The storage locations for the elements of a in a directly mapped cache are shown in Figure 6.6. Matrix elements that are brought in at a certain stage, without being used immediately, are used in subsequent iterations before the cache line holding these elements is overwritten by other cache lines.

In general, the dimension of the matrix is not a multiple of the cache line size. The cache lines that are needed in this case are shown in Figure 6.7.

The choice of the blocking parameter *lot* was obvious for the data set defined in Figure 6.5 and a cache whose characteristic parameters are declared in Figure 6.6.

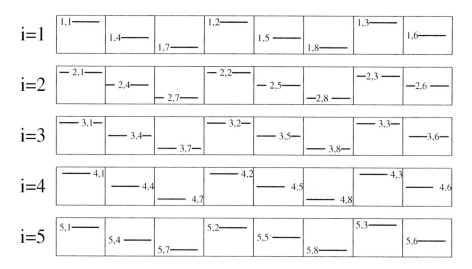

Figure 6.6: *Cache locations of the elements of a in the subroutine "rots." As in Figure 6.5, the leading dimension n of a is taken to be 12, the blocking parameter lot is 8. The first five iterations of the i loop are depicted. The order in which the elements are accessed in the j loop is obtained by reading the elements in the usual order, i.e., from left to right and then downwards. The figure assumes that one cache line (depicted as a box) can hold 4 array elements and that the entire cache (directly mapped) can hold 8 cache lines. We note that all cache lines are occupied after eight iterations of the j loop. Of the 32 words loaded during the first i iteration, only 8 are used in the same iteration. However, all the other 24 array elements are used in the following three i iterations. No other cache lines have to be loaded during these 3 i iterations. The elements are overwritten after 4 iterations of the i loop, but then they are no longer needed. In the absence of the j loop blocking, these 24 elements would be overwritten before used.*

In realistic cases, the determination of the largest possible value of *lot* is more difficult and is best done by the simulation program "cache_par" presented in section 6.7. This program can also be used to find an optimal leading dimension such that the effective cache size is equal (or nearly equal) to the physical one, as explained in section 6.8. The performance of a matrix transposition done in this way is shown in Figure 6.8. Even though cache thrashing is prevented in this case, we observe certain large matrix sizes where serious performance degradation occurs. This is due to TLB thrashing. Since the TLB behaves like a higher level cache, we can use the same simulation program "cache_par" to determine leading dimensions nd and blocking parameters *lot* that avoid both cache and TLB thrashing, as shown below. In contrast to square blocking, line blocking with respect to several cache levels does not lead to a larger number of loops. The number of loops is the same as for blocking with respect to a single level, only the leading dimension has to satisfy more constraints.

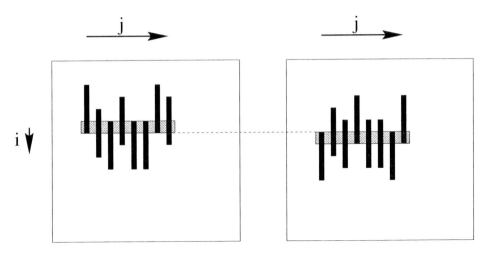

Figure 6.7: *Areas of the matrix a that are used during two successive iterations of the i loop in the subroutine "rots." The leading dimension n of a is not a multiple of the cache line size. The symbols used for the cache lines and elements accessed are the same as in Figure 6.5.*

```
        nd=n
111     continue
        call cache_par(ncache_line,ncache_size,nd,lotc)
        call cache_par(ntlb_line,ntlb_size,nd,lott)
c if we have frac of the physical cache and tlb size, we are satisfied
        frac=0.75d0
        if (lotc.ge.frac*ncache_size/ncache_line .and.
     &       lott.ge.frac*ntlb_size/ntlb_line) then
          goto 222
        endif
        nd=nd+1
        goto 111
222     continue
        lot=min(lotc,lott)
```

Once nd and lot are optimized for cache and TLB, we get good performance for all matrix sizes, as shown in Figure 6.9.

The performance data shown in Figures 6.3, 6.8, and 6.9 were actually obtained with unrolled versions of the subroutine "rots." Neglecting the tail section, which would insure correctness for odd values of n, this code has the following form:

```
        do 100,jj=1,n,lot
        do 100,i=1,n-1,2
        do 100,j=jj,min(n,jj+lot-1),2
          b(j+0,i+0)=a(i+0,j+0)
          b(j+0,i+1)=a(i+1,j+0)
          b(j+1,i+0)=a(i+0,j+1)
          b(j+1,i+1)=a(i+1,j+1)
100     continue
```

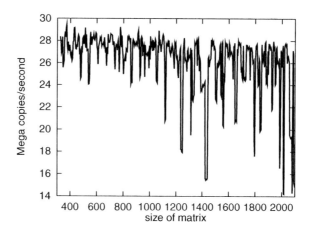

Figure 6.8: *Performance of a matrix transposition using one-dimensional blocking with an optimally adjusted leading dimension and a value of lot calculated by the cache simulation program "cache_par." For certain matrix sizes, serious performance degradation occurs due to TLB thrashing.*

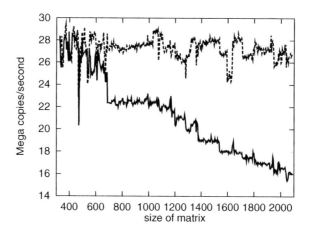

Figure 6.9: *The dashed lines show the performance of a matrix transposition using one-dimensional blocking where nd and lot were optimized with respect to both cache and TLB. The solid lines show the performance of the "DGETMO" matrix transposition subroutine from the ESSL library for the same leading dimensions nd.*

The fact that in this unrolled version we are referencing the array elements $a(i + 0, j + 0)$ and $a(i + 1, j + 0)$ suggests that we might actually use data belonging to two adjacent cache lines. The referenced array elements could even belong to two adjacent pages, an unlikely possibility that we choose to neglect. In all the tests presented in this section, we have determined nd and lot such that one associativity class of the cache can be filled up to a certain fraction of its physical capacity. In the case in which two adjacent cache lines are accessed in one loop iteration, the second cache line can always be stored in another associativity class. The remaining two associativity classes are, roughly speaking, reserved for the two data streams of the input array b ($b(*, i)$ and $b(*, i + 1)$), each having a stride-1 access pattern. Using two associativity classes for the input array b seems to be a waste. Its cache lines could, in principle, be overwritten immediately after being used. However, since we have no influence over which elements are overwritten (the least recently used policy in general determines that), we have to let these array elements age sufficiently in cache before they can be overwritten by useful new data. It is obvious that for this kind of memory access optimization, it is very convenient to have a larger number of associativity classes, such as the four-way associative cache of the IBM Power2 series that was used for these tests.

The optimization techniques presented here are well beyond what a compiler can do. No compiler can determine optimal leading dimensions nd, nor change the leading dimensions in a program. Similarly, no compiler can determine the blocking parameter lot, since the leading dimension may not be known at compile time.

The performance of one-dimensional blocking is limited by two factors. Since we have transformed a data access pattern with no locality into one with spatial data locality, the performance cannot exceed the stride-1 performance shown in Figure 6.1. The best possible performance is reached depending upon whether the innermost loop is long enough, i.e., the blocking parameter lot is big enough. The maximum value of the blocking parameter with respect to one memory hierarchy level is given by the number of slots available on that level, by which we mean the number of basic units such as cache lines or pages that the level can accommodate. The overall blocking parameter lot equals the smallest blocking parameter of all the cache levels. On an IBM 590, each associativity class of the cache and the TLB has 256 slots. Loops of length 256 give reasonably good performance. For matrix transposition, the performance shown in Figure 6.9 is close to the one obtained for stride-1 data access depicted in Figure 6.1. On the Digital AU433, the TLB has only 64 entries, which leads to loops too short for good performance in matrix transposition.

6.11   Prefetching

As mentioned repeatedly in this book, frequently the CPU of a RISC machine is not fed fast enough with data from memory. There are two possible reasons that can give rise to this bottleneck. The first reason is that the memory bandwidth is not large enough for data to arrive at the required rate from main memory. If a program schedules one load per cycle but the bandwidth to main memory only allows one transfer every two cycles, that program will be slowed down by a factor of 2. Even if the bandwidth allows for the transfer of one item per cycle, there is a second reason why programs can be slowed down, the memory latency. If load instructions are scheduled briefly before the data item is needed, possible cache misses can cause the CPU to idle until the data arrives in registers. To avoid this effect, the data item has to be requested long before needed. If the time between the initial request and the use of the data can be bridged with other computations for which the operands are available, the CPU will not idle and good performance is obtained. To a certain extent the compiler tries to schedule loads way ahead. However, there are limits to what the compiler can do, mainly related to the number of available registers. If a data item is loaded long before it is needed, it will occupy a register during this entire period. The solution would be an instruction that transfers one or several cache lines from the main memory into cache. In this case, it is no longer necessary to schedule the load way ahead, but only slightly earlier (as explained in section 5.2) since the data will be in cache and no cache misses will occur. An instruction of this type is called a prefetch. Prefetch instructions are part of the instruction set of some RISC architectures, such as the Cray T3E and the SGI/MIPS. Prefetch instructions are not provided for in the specifications of commonly used programming languages. Nevertheless, on some machines they can be invoked from high-level programming languages such as Fortran. Even when present, the syntax and the implementation details of prefetch vary widely from one manufacturer to another leading to lack of portability. For this reason we will not provide any coding example using prefetching. The interested reader can consult the technical documentation of the vendor for more information. We just point out that some of the compilers, such as the SGI F77 compiler, invoked with high optimization levels, attempt to do prefetch at strategic places in the code.

Alternatively, prefetching can be implemented in hardware, for example, by using stream buffers [13]. Based on runtime information from the first few iterations of a loop, a prediction is made as to what cache line will be needed in subsequent iterations. These cache lines are then preloaded into the stream buffer, from which they can be transferred very rapidly in cache. Stream buffers work well for simple access patterns only, such as small and constant stride access.

The hardware prefetch on the IBM Power3 architecture allows for up to four streams of loads, but streams for stores are not provided for, surprisingly. Since no prefetch instruction exists, the compiler has to be tricked to issue prefetches for the loads. As an example, the code for initializing a long vector to 1 is

```
do 200,i=1,n-15,16
  x(i+0)=1.d0+zero*x(i)
  x(i+1)=1.d0
  x(i+2)=1.d0
  x(i+3)=1.d0
  x(i+4)=1.d0
  x(i+5)=1.d0
  x(i+6)=1.d0
  x(i+7)=1.d0
  x(i+8)=1.d0
  x(i+9)=1.d0
  x(i+10)=1.d0
  x(i+11)=1.d0
  x(i+12)=1.d0
  x(i+13)=1.d0
  x(i+14)=1.d0
  x(i+15)=1.d0
200 continue
```

hiding from the compiler the fact that "zero" has the value "0." In this way a load stream of stride 16 is created. Since the length of the cache line is 16 words, all the cache lines will be loaded by hardware prefetch and the program runs two times faster. Similarly, the bandwidth for copying large vectors can be improved. This trick was not used in Figure 6.1, where we only did a standard unrolling of the code.

The Cray T3E has a hardware prefetch unit using stream buffers, in addition to its software prefetch instruction. In contrast to the Power3 architecture, this hardware prefetch feeds the registers directly from memory, circumventing the cache. Four input and two output streams can be generated simultaneously.

6.12 Misalignment of data

Double precision floating point numbers are usually aligned in such a way that they start at a memory location that is a multiple of eight bytes. The load/store operations take advantage of this convention by always transferring sections of eight bytes. By using some awkward programming constructs it is possible to undo this alignment. When that happens, a load of a doubleword requires the load of two consecutive sections of eight bytes, making it twice as costly. Generally, compilers align data correctly. Some Fortran instructions, specifying exact memory locations for data, can prevent the compiler from doing the alignment. One example of such instructions are the common blocks. By having a four-byte integer number listed first in the common block in the code below, all of the following eight-byte elements of the vector a will be misaligned. The performance of this routine is improved by a factor of 2 when using the correct alignment, namely, "common /data/ a,n ."

```
      subroutine lngth(tt)
      implicit real*8 (a-h,o-z)
      parameter(nx=2**12)
      dimension a(nx)
      common /data/ n,a

      tt=0.d0
      do 100,j=1,n
        tt=tt+a(j)*a(j)
100   continue

      return
      end
```

Another source of misalignment is the Fortran90 derived data type together with the "sequence" attribute. It prevents the compiler from arranging different data types within a derived data type in an optimal way. Most compilers issue warning messages when detecting misalignments.

Chapter 7

Miscellaneous Optimizations

7.1 Balancing the load of the functional units

Most CPUs consist of several independent functional units. The slowest unit can limit the speed of all other units. One example of such an imbalance is when out of cache data is accessed with large strides. In this case, the load/store unit is responsible for the slowdown, since it services all the cache and TLB misses. Another example is when the floating point unit calculates some expensive special function on a few operands only.

In some cases it is possible to organize a program in such a way that more than one functional unit, is simultaneously involved in work on a heavy workload. In this way, the bottleneck is alleviated and performance increases accordingly. As an example, when a gather operation

```
        do 100,i=1,n
100       x(i)=y(ind(i))
```

and a calculation of a square root on a vector of the same length n are present in a program

```
        do 200,i=1,n
200       a(i)=sqrt(b(i))
```

the merging of the two in a single loop will have the desired effect.

```
        do 300,i=1,n
          a(i)=sqrt(b(i))
300       x(i)=y(ind(i))
```

7.2 Accessing the instructions

Before the start of a program, the entire instruction sequence representing the program in machine language form is stored in the main memory. To speed up the access of the CPU to these instructions, a separate instruction cache is generally present. If two cache levels exist, then the second-level cache is usually used for both data and instructions. Concerning the access of the CPU to the instructions, issues very similar to those related to data access are encountered. However, things are considerably less transparent since, in general, the size of the instruction stack representing a certain portion of a program, such as a loop, is not known. Therefore, optimizations are difficult to implement. Fortunately, in most cases this is not necessary. On most machines the first-level instruction cache is large enough to house large loops. Problems may be encountered only on machines with a very small instruction cache, such as the DEC ALPHA EV5. In such a case, attempting to reduce the code size may be in order, for instance, by disabling loop unrolling and blocking transformations that increase the code size.

7.3 I/O: Writing to and reading from files

Disks can be considered as the highest level in the memory hierarchy. Access to disk is significantly slower than access to memory. 1/0 (input/output) operations, where data is read from or written to a file residing on a disk, are therefore very costly. As a rough rule of thumb, I/O operations cost a few hundred cycles. The most important optimization rule is to keep I/O to a strict minimum. If large I/O operations are unavoidable, unformatted I/O should be preferred over formatted I/O. Unformatted I/O saves calls to the library that translates data from binary form to character form with respect to base 10. Again, as a rough rule of thumb, unformatted I/O is a few times faster than formatted I/O. In addition, the resulting unformatted files are approximately half the size of the corresponding formatted file.

7.4 Memory fragmentation in Fortran90

Fortran90 allows for the allocation and deallocation of memory at runtime. Under certain circumstances, the effective capacity of the physical memory is exhausted even though the total allocated memory is smaller than the size of the memory. This is called memory fragmentation, and its impact is very similar to cache thrashing, only applied to memory.

Figures 7.1 and 7.2 illustrate several hypothetical states of memory utilization in a Fortran90 program. In the first stage, six blocks were allocated that completely fill the physical memory. In the second stage, blocks 1, 3 and 5 are deallocated. In the third stage, a block is allocated that is twice as big as the original blocks. Since the newly allocated block is bigger, it does not fit into any of the "holes" left by deallocating the smaller original blocks. Therefore, the block is assigned a location in the virtual address space that is outside the physical memory and corresponds to the disk space.

Two scenarios are possible, depending on the relative size of the blocks compared to the page size. When the blocks are sizable, the new block extends over several pages and needs to be chunked in a number of pieces in order to fit in the slots

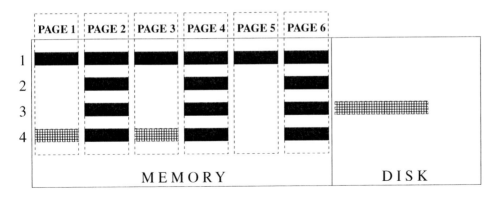

Figure 7.1: *Four stages (denoted by 1, 2, 3, 4) of the execution of a Fortran90 program described in the text.*

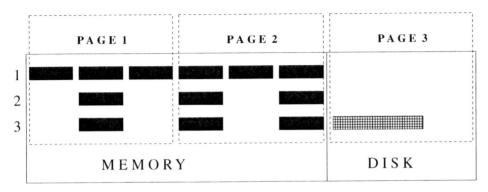

Figure 7.2: *Same as Figure 7.1, under the assumption that the size of the allocated blocks is small compared to the page size. Memory fragmentation will result.*

made available by deallocating the original blocks. This is shown in Figure 7.1. The TLB will keep track of this process as described in section 2.5.

Paging can become severe if the original blocks were small, i.e., if they extend over only a few pages or even a fraction of a page. The latter effect is indicated in Figure 7.2 by making the unrealistic assumption that only two pages fit into the physical memory. In this way, the blocks are necessarily small compared to the page size. Excessive paging that can bring the program to a near standstill will result from such a scenario. To avoid this possibility, repeated allocation and deallocation of amounts of memory that are small compared to the page size should be avoided in a Fortran90 program.

7.5 Optimizations for vector architectures

Even though some similarities exist between the architectural features of RISC and vector computers, the optimization techniques are in general quite different. A

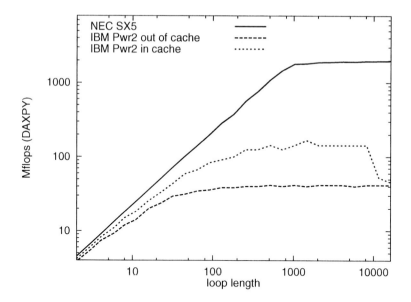

Figure 7.3: *Performance of the BLAS DAXPY routine as a function of its loop length on the NEC SX5 vector machine and the IBM Power2 RISC workstation. The absolute performance is always larger on the vector machine, although longer loop lengths are necessary to achieve a significant percentage of the peak speed.*

program highly tuned for a RISC machine will not run fast on a vector machine and vice versa. In this section we will briefly describe a few general principles for obtaining good performance on a vector machine. We refer the reader to [23] for a comprehensive discussion of vector-specific optimizations.

The basic rule for efficiency is to have very long inner loops without any if statements and dependencies. Even though this is similar to the conclusions we arrived at for the case of superscalars, differences exist. On a vector machine, it is really important to have very long inner loops. While superscalar machines run at high speed for loops of length 10 to 100, loop lengths of the order of 100 to 1000 are needed on a vector machine to obtain roughly the same fraction of the peak speed. This is illustrated in Figure 7.3.

The elimination of dependencies is more difficult on vector architectures. To illustrate this, let's go back to our familiar example of the calculation of the Euclidian norm of a vector.

```
        subroutine lngth(n,a,tt)
        implicit real*8 (a-h,o-z)
        dimension a(n)

        tt=0.d0
        do 100,j=1,n
          tt=tt+a(j)*a(j)
100     continue

        return
        end
```

The basic problem with this loop on a vector is the same as on a RISC machine. Succeeding loop iterations are dependent, with the effect of pipeline stalls in every iteration. The solution for RISC was in unrolling the loop to a moderate depth, such as 4, and then creating four independent execution streams by introducing four independent scalar accumulation variables. Since the maximum length of the vector registers is typically 64 or 128, we could expect that the depth of unrolling is that large here. However, unrolling with scalar variables will not work. To get good performance on a vector machine we need simple inner loops with independent vector operations instead of scalar operations. A slightly modified unrolling scheme, reminiscent of blocking, gives the optimal structure:

```
      do 15,j=1,lot
        w(j)=0.d0
15    continue

      do 25,jj=0,n-lot,lot
      do 25,j=1,lot
        w(j)=w(j)+a(jj+j)*a(jj+j)
25    continue

      tt=0.d0
      do 35,j=1,lot
        tt=tt+w(j)
35    continue
```

The blocking parameter lot should be at least as large as the vector register length. In addition, we introduce a work array w of size lot. For simplicity we assumed that n is a multiple of lot. If that is not the case, the remaining elements have to be processed one by one in a scalar fashion. It is clear that this method is worthwhile only if the length of the vector a is much larger than lot.

With vectorization being disabled in the original version "lngth," the performance on a Cray C90 is just 20 Mflops. In the vectorizable form, obtained by the transformations just discussed, the performance jumps to 880 Mflops for long enough loop lengths. The good news here is that this transformation is done automatically by vectorizing compilers at the default optimization level. The compiler technology for vectorizing compilers is in general more mature than for superscalar architectures. Automatic vectorization done by such compilers leads to good performance levels for a wide range of code complexities.

Since data locality is not an issue on vector machines without caches, loop blocking is not necessary. On the contrary, blocking reduces the length of the inner loops and leads to performance degradation. For the same reason, loop unrolling should be avoided. In addition to the shorter loop lengths, unrolling has a second detrimental effect in that the number of required registers is increased. The number of vector registers is rather small, much smaller than the 32 registers found on most RISC machines. Unrolled loops can lead to vector register spilling. There is only one exception in which modest loop unrolling can help. If a loop is load/store bound, the unrolling can improve the ratio of floating point to load/store operations without vector register spilling. Older vector machines, such as the Cray C90 and

T90, can do four loads and two stores per cycle in vector mode. This is just the amount needed to sustain a DAXPY operation through the dual multiply and add functional pipelines. On some newer machines, this load/store throughput is smaller.

The absence of data locality requirements on a vector machine frequently leads to loop orders that are different from the ones on RISC computers. A well-known example is the matrix-vector multiplication. On a RISC machine the inner loop should be a scalar product (i.e., the DDOT j loop in the code below) to avoid loading and storing $y(i)$ in each iteration. On the vector machine the optimal loop order is the reversed one, in order to eliminate any dependencies.

```
do j=1,n2
do i=1,n1
  y(i)=y(i)+a(j,i)*x(j)
enddo
enddo
```

One rule that incidentally applies to both vector and cache architectures is that leading dimensions that are high powers of 2 should be avoided. On a cache architecture, observing this rule minimizes conflict cache misses, on a vector machine it avoids hitting the same memory bank before its recovery time. The technique to eliminate such leading dimensions, discussed in section 6.6, is applicable to vector machines too.

Chapter 8

Optimization of Parallel Programs

The primary motivation for using parallel computers is to obtain faster turnaround time for the computations. In addition, parallel machines offer access to more memory than single processors. Achieving high efficiency on parallel machines is closely related to the choice of algorithms and to optimal data distribution among the processing elements. As interprocessor communication is the costliest component of any parallel algorithm, algorithms well suited for parallelism are those that can be divided into relatively independent subproblems that can be solved without much data exchange. Such algorithms are generically called "coarse-grained." Algorithms of this type are not known for all computational problems. Another essential ingredient for parallel efficiency is the optimization of the serial code, already extensively discussed. In fact, parallel optimization should be done only after the serial program is optimal. This strategy is likely to lead to best parallel performance and avoids artificially inflated speedup numbers.

In this chapter we will first discuss metrics for parallel performance and then offer some guidelines on how to optimize parallel programs.

8.1 Ideal and observed speedup

One measure of parallel efficiency is the "parallel speedup," which tells how many times faster a program runs on a parallel machine compared to a single processor of the same type. If N is the number of processors (or processing elements), the ideal speedup S_i is

$$S_i = N.$$

The ideal speedup is a theoretical limit, not attainable except for a very small subset of real problems called "embarrassingly parallel." Such a program typically requires just the distribution and collection of some data at the beginning and at the end of the run. In practice, the real speedup S_r is smaller than the ideal speedup. Several definitions of the real speedup exist [30]. Given the different metrics, reporting of speedup needs to be done carefully. We will discuss here two of these definitions, namely, *strong* and *weak scalability*. Strong scalability means that the number of processors increases while problem size is fixed. Therefore, the workload per processor decreases. Weak scalability implies that both the problem size and the number of processors increase. The workload per processor is constant or can even increase if the overall workload grows faster than linearly with respect to the size of the computational problem. High speedups are easier to obtain for the weak scaling case.

Two main factors prevent a code from attaining the ideal speedup S_i. The first one is related to the fact that, in any program, nonparallelizable segments are present. Amdahl's law, discussed below, gives the speedup that can be expected as a function of the fraction of the workload that is parallel. The second limiting factor comes from the fact that access to global memory involves interprocessor communication and therefore is rather slow. Given that, not even the speedup predicted by Amdahl's law can be obtained in practice.

If we denote by f the fraction of a code that is parallelizable, then the total parallel execution time will be given by (serial time) $\times (f/N + (1 - f))$. The speedup is consequently given by

$$S_a = 1/(1 - f + f/N).$$

This simple upper bound for the speedup is known as Amdahl's law. The Amdahl speedup S_a is plotted for several values of f in Figure 8.1. Unless a large fraction of the code can be parallelized, the speedups are limited to fairly small values. In fact, since $S_a < 1/(1 - f)$, S_a will never exceed this value regardless of how many processors are used. Amdahl's law states a situation of diminishing returns. If a code has a sizable serial component, adding more computational power by increasing the number of processors is not going to cure the problem. Instead, the solution involves using algorithms better suited to parallel computation, or at least restructuring the code in such a way that the parallelizable fraction f increases.

Actually, we are interested in the "observed speedup" S_o, which is obtained by experiment. By measuring the elapsed time of the serial program, and the elapsed time for its parallel version, we can write:

$$S_o = \text{(elapsed time for serial version)}/\text{(elapsed time of parallel version)}.$$

S_o includes the effect on the code's performance from all real-life factors affecting performance, such as communication for data transfer between different processors. The observed speedup S_o is therefore always lower than the Amdahl limit. Particular care has to be given when measuring S_o. For example, a so-called superlinear speedup S_o, larger than the Amdahl limit, can be obtained when cache misses are reduced due to smaller data sizes per processor as the number of processors is increased. This is a clear indication that the serial version was not well optimized. Speedups are shown in Figure 8.1 for several hypothetical programs. Note that, in the Amdahl case, the speedup will saturate at the Amdahl limit $1/(1 - f)$, whereas in a real-life program the speedup will actually start to degrade when lots

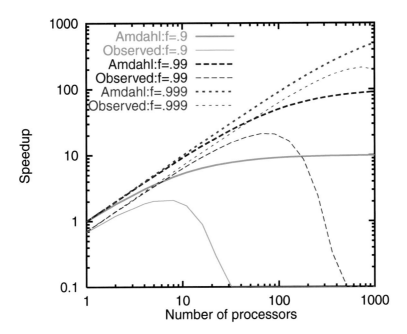

Figure 8.1: *The Amdahl and the observed speedup for three hypothetical codes that have serial fractions of* 10, 1 *and* .1 *percent.*

of processors are added, as the communication overhead becomes the dominating factor.

8.2 Message passing libraries

Message passing architectures utilize communication libraries such as MPI or PVM (parallel virtual machine) for exchanging nonlocal data (i.e., data residing in the memory belonging to another processor). Detailed information on these libraries can be found on the Web (http://www-unix.mcs.anl.gov/mpi/index.htm, http://www.erc.msstate.edu/labs/hpcl/projects/mpi/, http://www.epm.ornl.gov/pvm/) or in the printed literature [28, 14].

The MPI message passing library has been adopted as a de facto standard for communication by the scientific community. A parallel program using MPI is portable and, since nearly all manufacturers have an MPI implementation that is optimized for their specific communication hardware, it gives good communication performance compared to nonoptimized communication libraries. The MPI library not only contains basic point-to-point routines, where two processors are involved in communication, but also a wide range of global communication routines where all or subsets of processors are involved in a concerted communication step. Examples of global communication routines are global reduction sums, where some quantity calculated in all participating processors is summed up in one processor, or data from one processor is broadcast to all the others in the group.

Whenever possible, usage of one single MPI routine is preferable over using several lower level routines, such as when attempting to build a global communication routine from point-to-point routines. The MPI global communication kernel is likely to be more efficient, and programming is easier too.

Latency effects can be reduced by concatenating several messages into a single one before sending it. In this way, several calls to a communication kernel can be replaced by a single one. In point-to-point communications, nonblocking communication routines are generally more efficient than blocking ones. Nonblocking routines allow the processor to continue with other useful work when the message cannot be sent immediately, while in the case of blocking routines the processor is idle until the completion of the communication.

The use of nonblocking communication in Fortran90 codes can, under some circumstances, be error prone. If the send is done from within a subroutine where the send-buffer is an allocated array, the send-buffer can be destroyed by deallocation if the subroutine exits before the send is completed. A similar, perhaps more insidious, problem can occur if a noncontiguous array section is passed, Fortran90 style, to a MPI routine. Since the MPI routines are Fortran77 style and assume that the input arrays are contiguous, the compiler must create a temporary array into which it concatenates the noncontiguous data. After the nonblocking MPI routine returns control to the calling program, the temporary array will probably be deallocated before the communication actually takes place.

The MPI-2 standard provides for "remote memory access" or "one-sided communication" routines (MPI_GET, MPI_PUT) that are very similar to the CRAY SHMEM routines. While standard MPI routines require matching operations between the sender and the receiver, these routines are one-sided, i.e., all the transfer parameters are known only to the sender or the receiver, but not to both of them. Hence, they have the potential of being more efficient. In addition, they can simplify the code structure.

8.3   Data locality

Data locality is of utmost importance for high parallel performance. All the data locality concepts discussed in the serial part can be taken over in a straightforward way to the parallel case if we just think of the global memory of a distributed memory machine as the highest level in the memory hierarchy of the computer. Having good data locality means, in the case of a distributed memory parallel machine, that most of the data that is needed by one processor is available in the memory physically attached to that processor. Since the access to data located on other processors necessitates interprocessor communication, good data locality will minimize this slow component of the program. In general, it is a good practice to try to predict whether it is not faster to replicate some results on all the processors, at the price of more floating point arithmetic, instead of communicating them. In the case of the Cray T3E, for which the effective bandwidth was plotted in Figure 2.5, we see that we can hope under the most favorable circumstances for a bandwidth of approximately 40 Mwords/second. Since the Cray T3E processor runs at 500

MHz, this means that we can feed one double precision number from the network into the processor every 12 cycles. In many cases, the calculation of each number takes less than 12 cycles. This advice holds true on other parallel machines too, as the ratio of the cost for sending numbers to that of calculating them is in the same range.

8.4 Load balancing

The concept of load balancing is a simple one, but its effect on performance is significant. Ideally, in a parallel program the distribution of the total workload among the different processing elements would be perfectly uniform. If the distribution is not balanced, then some processing elements will idle while others are still doing work. For example, if one processing element has a workload that is twice as big as the workload of all the other processing elements, then all these processing elements will idle half of the time and the overall efficiency is nearly cut in half compared with the case when perfect load balancing can be achieved. The strategy for distributing the workload is usually motivated by the problem to be solved. For example, in calculations on a homogeneous grid, a likely data distribution is the assignment of a subgrid (each containing the same number of grid points) to each processing element. In molecular dynamics calculations, we usually assign a certain number of atoms to each processor. In this case, it may turn out that the workload associated with different atoms varies considerably because the number of nearest neighbors could be different for each atom. In this case, a "pool of tasks" administered by a master processor scheme could be more advantageous. The master processor hands out tasks to each worker processor. Once the worker processor sends back its result, it immediately gets the next task from the master.

8.5 Minimizing the surface-to-volume ratio in grid-based methods

Many scientific and engineering codes are using grid-based techniques such as finite-difference and finite-element. Let us consider the case of a structured grid, such as the two-dimensional Cartesian grid shown in Figure 8.2. From load balancing considerations, it follows that each processor should own the same number of grid points. However, there are many ways to satisfy this constraint, as shown in Figure 8.2. Let's assume that we employ a stencil of the type

$$W(i,j) = \frac{1}{4}\left(V(i-1,j) + V(i+1,j) + V(i,j-1) + V(i,j+1)\right). \tag{8.1}$$

This stencil requires neighboring grid points, located on other processors for the grid points on the boundary, as illustrated in Figure 8.3. This requires communication. Hence it follows that the amount of communication per processor is proportional to the surface of its associated subvolume, whereas the work done by each processor is proportional to the volume. Keeping communication to a minimum requires the

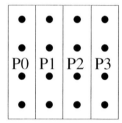 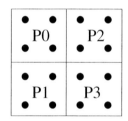

Figure 8.2: *Two ways to equally distribute* 16 *grid points on four processors. The subdivision into squares on the right is more efficient since its surface (circumference in the two-dimensional case) is smaller.*

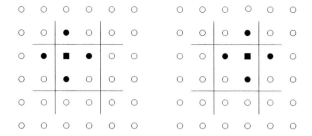

Figure 8.3: *A grid partitioning where four grid points (shown by circles) are associated with one processor. On the left, all the points needed to update the upper left grid point (denoted by a square), according to* (8.1), *are shown by black dots. The same thing applies on the right for the upper right grid point.*

minimization of the surface-to-volume ratio of the grid partitioning. If we have rectangular subvolumes of side-length l_x and l_y, the surface S is $S = 2l_x + 2l_y$ and the volume V is $V = l_x l_y$. Minimizing the surface under the constraint of a constant volume gives (by elementary calculus rules) $l_x^2 = l_y^2 = V$. Hence a square is optimal. In the same way, we can show that a cube is the best orthorhombic box in the three-dimensional case. For a given number of grid points and processors it is not possible, in general, to choose subvolumes that are exact squares or cubes, but we should strive for subgrids that are similar to these optimal shapes.

Exercise: Prove that a cubic box has the best volume-to-surface ratio of all orthorhombic volumes.

8.6   Coarse-grain parallelism against fine-grain parallelism

A coarse-grain parallel program is one in which a relatively large computational subtask is assigned to each processor. Each processing element will do computations for quite a while before entering a communication step. Otherwise stated, the

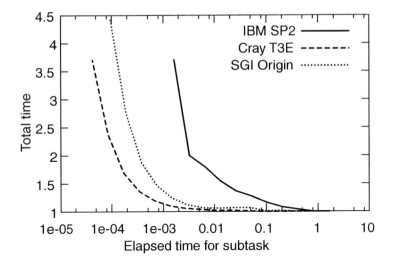

Figure 8.4: *The total elapsed time versus the time length of the subtask for a constant workload. The timings are shown for 64-processor configurations on IBM SP2, Cray T3E and SGI Origin2000 computers.*

computation/communication ratio is large. Fine-grain parallelism is the opposite case, involving short computation periods frequently interrupted by communication. Fine-grain parallelism is typically obtained by parallelizing at the loop level. Fine-grain programs can achieve reasonable speedups on shared memory machines, but not on large distributed memory architectures. Therefore, obtaining good speedups on a wide range of parallel computers requires coarse-grain algorithms.

The suitability of several parallel computers for fine-grain applications is shown in Figure 8.4. A large computational task was artificially subdivided into subtasks, whose length is shown on the x-axis. On an ideal parallel computer, where communication is infinitely fast, the total elapsed time shown on the y-axis would be a constant.

The communication requirements for the program ("grain_mpi.f," listed in section A.5 of the appendix) are minimal, consisting of a broadcast followed by a global reduction sum. In realistic programs, the communication requirements will likely be much larger, hence the smallest possible grain size that gives a reasonable performance in our example will be a lower bound for any realistic application. Very large differences can be seen for the three parallel computers tested. On the IBM SP2, grain sizes smaller than a tenth of a second lead already to serious performance deterioration, whereas we can go down to grain sizes of 1/1000th of a second on the Cray T3E. The same trend was seen in Figure 2.10, where a global data transposition was timed on the same machines.

One partial exception to the rule of largest possible grain size in parallel programs is a program based on the master–slave paradigm. Load balancing can suffer if the individual tasks handed out to the slaves are too large. Another exception are "wavefront" algorithms, in which large subgrid sizes lead to low processor utilization. A detailed discussion of these algorithms is presented in [18].

8.7   Adapting parallel programs to the computer topology

Communication can be made more efficient by adapting it to the network topology. For example, a sensible data decomposition for a three-dimensional grid problem on a machine with a three-dimensional torus network is the assignment of subgrids to processors in such a way that grids that are neighbors in physical space are topological neighbors too. In this way, contention for the routers is minimized on any network. Some factors that need to be considered before such optimizations are attempted are:

- Programs tuned in this way will perform worse on machines with different topologies.

- Communication software overhead tends to diminish the influence of the topology. Even on the Cray T3E, a parallel machine with a direct network (torus), topological effects are usually small. This can easily be verified by running a program on subsets of processors forming topologically different configurations. The timing fluctuations from one run to another using different processor configurations, without any change in the data distribution, are an indication of the importance of topological effects.

For these reasons this type of parallel optimization is not worthwhile in most cases.

Chapter 9

Case Studies

All the programs discussed up to now were chosen for their simplicity. In this section we will optimize some real and consequently more complex applications using all the performance tuning knowledge acquired in the preceding sections. We will stress the important initial phase that has to take place before starting to write a program. This precoding phase of application development is where the design of the data and code structure is decided.

9.1 Matrix-vector multiplication

Highly optimized implementations of the BLAS subroutine DGEMV performing this linear algebra operation exist in many scientific libraries provided by vendors. This way, we will be able to compare our optimization achievements with the results of these highly optimized libraries. Given its relative simplicity, this example also illustrates the limited capabilities of high-level compiler optimizations.

The unoptimized matrix-vector multiplication subroutine has the following form:

```
        subroutine mxvs(m,nd,n,a,x,y)
        implicit real*8 (a-h,o-z)
        dimension a(nd,m),x(m),y(nd)

        do 2000,i=1,n
        do 2000,j=1,m
          y(i)=y(i)+a(i,j)*x(j)
2000    continue

        return
        end
```

The path to follow for optimizing this routine, based on the principles learned so far, is quite straightforward. First optimization consists of unrolling the i loop to exhibit more parallelism and to reduce the number of loads of the array element $x(j)$, as discussed in section 5.4. For large data sets, line blocking is necessary since we have a nonunit stride access of the matrix a in the innermost loop. Switching the

loop order would not be advisable, as it would increase the number of loads/stores.
In this case, $y(i)$ would have to be loaded and stored in each iteration. We target
the IBM Power2 architecture for the optimization of this program. We would like
to take advantage of its special load instruction allowing the load of two adjacent
double precision words in a single cycle. This necessitates unrolling the j loop to
a depth of 2. By unrolling the i loop to a depth of 8, 26 registers are needed, a
reasonable value. In contrast to all preceding examples, we have now added code
that handles the "leftover" parts of the unrolled loops for the case where the total
number of loop iterations is not a multiple of the unrolling depth. To find the
starting values of the counters js and is for these leftover loops, we take advantage
of the Fortran convention stipulating that a loop exits when its counter is larger
than its upper limit. Thus, when leaving the loop, the counters are set to the
correct starting value for the leftover loops. The hand-optimized version is listed
below.

```
        subroutine mxv(m,nd,n,lot,a,x,y)
        implicit real*8 (a-h,o-z)
        dimension a(nd,m),x(m),y(nd)

c line-blocking loop
        do 2000,jj=1,m,lot
           j0=jj
           j1=min(jj+lot-1,m)
c unrolled i loop
           do 200,i=1,n-7,8
             t1=y(i+0)
             t2=y(i+1)
             t3=y(i+2)
             t4=y(i+3)
             t5=y(i+4)
             t6=y(i+5)
             t7=y(i+6)
             t8=y(i+7)
c unrolled inner j loop
             do 100,j=j0,j1-1,2
               t1=t1+a(i+0,j+0)*x(j+0)+a(i+0,j+1)*x(j+1)
               t2=t2+a(i+1,j+0)*x(j+0)+a(i+1,j+1)*x(j+1)
               t3=t3+a(i+2,j+0)*x(j+0)+a(i+2,j+1)*x(j+1)
               t4=t4+a(i+3,j+0)*x(j+0)+a(i+3,j+1)*x(j+1)
               t5=t5+a(i+4,j+0)*x(j+0)+a(i+4,j+1)*x(j+1)
               t6=t6+a(i+5,j+0)*x(j+0)+a(i+5,j+1)*x(j+1)
               t7=t7+a(i+6,j+0)*x(j+0)+a(i+6,j+1)*x(j+1)
               t8=t8+a(i+7,j+0)*x(j+0)+a(i+7,j+1)*x(j+1)
100          continue
c remainder of j loop
             js=j
             do 110,j=js,j1
               t1=t1+a(i+0,j+0)*x(j+0)
               t2=t2+a(i+1,j+0)*x(j+0)
               t3=t3+a(i+2,j+0)*x(j+0)
               t4=t4+a(i+3,j+0)*x(j+0)
               t5=t5+a(i+4,j+0)*x(j+0)
               t6=t6+a(i+5,j+0)*x(j+0)
               t7=t7+a(i+6,j+0)*x(j+0)
```

Table 9.1: *Performance results (in Mflops) for a matrix-vector multiplication on an IBM 590. We used the xlf compiler version 4.02. Compared here are the results of the hand-optimized version, the IBM ESSL library, a medium-level compiler optimization ($-O2$ $-qarch = pwr2$) and a high-level compiler optimization ("$-O3$ $-qarch = pwr2$ $-qhot$"). The leading dimension of the matrix a was determined by the simulation routine "cache_par" from section 6.8.*

	Hand opt.	ESSL	Compiler, medium opt.	Compiler, high opt.
In cache	255	220	65	145
Out of cache	130	160	4	4

```
              t8=t8+a(i+7,j+0)*x(j+0)
110           continue
              y(i+0)=t1
              y(i+1)=t2
              y(i+2)=t3
              y(i+3)=t4
              y(i+4)=t5
              y(i+5)=t6
              y(i+6)=t7
              y(i+7)=t8
200        continue
c remainder of i loop
           is=i
           do 220,i=is,n
            t1=y(i+0)
            do 121,j=j0,j1
             t1=t1+a(i+0,j+0)*x(j+0)
121         continue
            y(i+0)=t1
220        continue
2000    continue

        return
        end
```

A most interesting question is how well the compiler can optimize such a relatively simple code, compared to the performance of the hand-optimized code and the library subroutine. Various performance results are shown in Table 9.1.

For in-cache data, the hand-optimized version runs close to peak speed. ESSL's "DGEMV" routine, highly tuned for this architecture, also achieves very good performance running at 220 Mflops. The speed obtained by compiling the unoptimized version with medium-level optimization is much lower. Even when using the most aggressive compiler optimization levels, we get no more than 145 Mflops. The situation becomes even worse for out-of-cache data sets. The compiler was unable to make any significant improvements leading to a speed of a mere 4 Mflops. Sarkar [27] proposed an explanation for this behavior. At the optimization level "$-O3$ $-qhot$" the compiler does, among other things, a simulation of the number of cache misses as a function of the dimensions of the array. Since in this subroutine the dimensions of the array are not given, the compiler cannot do any simulations. The situation changes dramatically when this information becomes available through a parameter statement.

```
subroutine mxvs(a,x,y)
implicit real*8 (a-h,o-z)
parameter(m=1000,n=1000,nd=1028)
...............
```

Now, with high optimization levels, the compiler performs beneficial code transformation, achieving a speed of 110 Mflops. This is more reasonable, although still significantly lower than the performance of the hand-optimized version or the ESSL library. Moreover, explicitly providing dimension statements within a subroutine is against the basic concept of a subroutine. The purpose should be to optimize and use subroutines for matrices of any size.

The superb performance of the ESSL library for out of cache data deserves some explanations. As described in [3], the ESSL library uses prefetching techniques that are adapted to the smallest details of the architecture. These techniques take advantage of the exact order in which entries in a cache line become available after a cache miss. These kinds of prefetch techniques cannot be implemented in Fortran, but require assembler coding.

Optimization is both a science and a craft. The transformations we did to hand-optimize this routine were certainly quite logical, thus representing the science component of this work. To exemplify its craftlike side we propose the following scenario. Let's think of an even better way to unroll the j loop, to a depth of 10 instead of 8. In this case, 32 register are required and one should obtain the best possible ratio of floating point operations to loads/stores. However, this is not true. Using all of the 32 registers gives less flexibility to the compiler and prevents it from doing certain optimizations. The speed obtained is lower for in-cache and for out of cache data.

9.2   Sparse matrix-vector multiplication

Sparse matrix operations are found in a wide range of applications in science and engineering. Unfortunately, the speed obtained in sparse matrix operations is, in general, much lower than the peak speed of any RISC architecture.

The SPARSKIT package (http://www.cs.unm.edu/Research/arpa/SPARSKIT/sparskit.html) is widely used for transformations between different data structures used for storing sparse matrices and for doing basic linear algebra operations. We have listed below the main loops of the "AMUX" routine of this package, doing a matrix-vector multiplication for a sparse matrix a stored in a "compressed sparse row" format.

```
      do 100 i = 1,n
c
c compute the inner product of row i with vector x
c
      t = 0.0d0
```

```
          do 99 k=ia(i), ia(i+1)-1
            t = t + a(k)*x(ja(k))
99          continue
c
c store result in y(i)
c
            y(i) = t
100       continue
```

The innermost loop is similar to a scalar product. For a scalar product of two dense vectors, up to half of peak speed for in-cache data can be expected on a RISC machine. This type of scalar product has two features that will significantly reduce this performance expectation. For very sparse matrices, the inner loop will be short and, because x is indirectly indexed, we have one additional load compared to the case of dense matrix-vector products. Since the loop is load/store bound, the additional load will have an immediate influence on its performance. Thus, the new performance expectation is roughly one-fourth of the peak speed, provided that the loop is unrolled so that four independent streams are present. The exact speed will depend on the actual structure of the sparse matrix a. If the data do not fit in cache (a, x, y and ja should be in cache at the same time), the situation worsens considerably. Consecutively accessed elements of x will, in general, belong to different cache lines. Thus, practically each memory reference to x will cause a capacity cache miss. The only way to bring performance to an acceptable level in this case is by exploiting the structure of the matrix, whenever present. Such changes will always be based on an in-depth understanding of the specific problem, and therefore general recipes cannot be given. For illustration purposes, we will briefly describe some solutions that we found useful in some of our applications.

Frequently, the matrix exhibits a block structure; i.e., it is composed of submatrices. The block structure arises naturally in many applications. In finite element calculations more than one shape function is commonly used per grid point. In quantum mechanical calculations many basis functions are utilized for each atom. Both scenarios lead to such a block structure. In the case of block submatrices, a restructuring of the sparse representation of the whole matrix is possible. We index each subblock instead of each individual element. Assuming that our matrix consists of 4×4 blocks only, the sparse matrix-vector multiply looks as follows:

```
      dimension x(4,n),y(4,n),a(4,4,*)

      do 100 i = 1,n
        t1 = 0.d0
        t2 = 0.d0
        t3 = 0.d0
        t4 = 0.d0
        do 99 k=ia(i), ia(i+1)-1
          kk=ja(k)
          t1=t1+a(1,1,k)*x(1,kk)+a(1,2,k)*x(2,kk)+a(1,3,k)*x(3,kk)+a(1,4,k)*x(4,kk)
          t2=t2+a(2,1,k)*x(1,kk)+a(2,2,k)*x(2,kk)+a(2,3,k)*x(3,kk)+a(2,4,k)*x(4,kk)
          t3=t3+a(3,1,k)*x(1,kk)+a(3,2,k)*x(2,kk)+a(3,3,k)*x(3,kk)+a(3,4,k)*x(4,kk)
          t4=t4+a(4,1,k)*x(1,kk)+a(4,2,k)*x(2,kk)+a(4,3,k)*x(3,kk)+a(4,4,k)*x(4,kk)
        99 continue
        y(1,i) = t1
```

```
        y(2,i) = t2
        y(3,i) = t3
        y(4,i) = t4
100     continue
```

This loop has a much better structure for performance. Apart from having built in four independent streams, the ratio of floating point operations to loads/stores is greatly improved. The number of capacity cache misses will be reduced by a factor of roughly 4, since the four consecutive array elements $x(1, kk)$, $x(2, kk)$, $x(3, kk)$ and $x(4, kk)$ belong to the same cache line. The number of references to a could be further reduced if each 4×4 block is a symmetric submatrix. In this case we can store only the upper triangle in compressed form.

Another possibility for restructuring comes from the fact that frequently the program can be organized such that more than one matrix-vector multiplication is executed at a time. Many iterative methods for solving linear equations or eigenvalue problems have "block versions," where work on several vectors at a time is performed. Let us assume, for simplicity, that we are working on four vectors at a time. The natural way to order the dimensions of these four vectors would be to group them as $x(n, 4)$. For best efficiency in this routine it is advisable to change the order of the dimensions to $x(4, n)$, which leads to the following multiplication routine:

```
        dimension x(4,n),y(4,n),a(*)

        do 100 i = 1,n
          t1 = 0.d0
          t2 = 0.d0
          t3 = 0.d0
          t4 = 0.d0
          do 99 k=ia(i), ia(i+1)-1
            kk=ja(k)
            t1=t1+a(k)*x(1,kk)
            t2=t2+a(k)*x(2,kk)
            t3=t3+a(k)*x(3,kk)
            t4=t4+a(k)*x(4,kk)
99        continue
          y(1,i) = t1
          y(2,i) = t2
          y(3,i) = t3
          y(4,i) = t4
100     continue
```

This loop structure has characteristics similar to that for the case of the 4×4 subblocks matrix presented above. Therefore, we get greatly improved performance, especially for out of cache data sets.

9.3   Two loops from a configuration interaction program

The configuration interaction (CI) method is a standard quantum chemistry method for electronic structure calculations of atoms and molecules. The number of configurations that are necessary for a high-accuracy description grows exponentially with the number of electrons. Both the memory and CPU time requirements are consequently very large in most calculations. The basic operation in a CI program is a matrix-vector multiplication, where the vector contains all the amplitudes of the different configurations. Even though the matrix is sparse, the number of non-zero elements is too large to be stored. Hence the matrix has to be calculated "on the fly"; i.e., each element is calculated from some auxiliary values in the matrix-vector multiplication routine at practically no extra cost. Two representative loop structures of a CI program for a four-electron system are listed below. In this initial version, the six loops in each structure were ordered in such a way that the innermost loops (100 and 200) are of the DDOT type (i.e., a scalar product is calculated). Because of the reduced number of loads/stores, this ordering is more efficient for matrix-vector multiplications on RISC machines than the alternative ordering in which the innermost loop is a DAXPY. A performance of 10 Mflops is obtained on an IBM Power2 workstation for $nstat=31$.

```
C y[ ii1 ii2 jj1 jj2 ] x[ ii1 ii2 j1 j2 ]
        do 1000,jj2=2,nstat
        do 1000,jj1= 1,jj2-1
        jy=ijnd(jj1,jj2)
        do 1000,ii2=2,nstat
        do 1000,ii1= 1,ii2-1
        iy=ijnd(ii1,ii2)
        ix=ijnd(ii1,ii2)
        do 100,j2=2,nstat
        do 100,j1= 1, j2-1
        jx=ijnd( j1, j2)
        t1 = t1 + qq( j1,jj1, j2,jj2)*x(ix,jx)
        t1 = t1 - qq( j1,jj2, j2,jj1)*x(ix,jx)
100     continue
        y(iy,jy) = t1
1000    continue

C y[ ii1 ii2 jj1 jj2 ] x[ ii1 i2 jj1 j2 ]
        do 2000,jj2=2,nstat
        do 2000,jj1= 1,jj2-1
        jy=ijnd(jj1,jj2)
        do 2000,ii2=2,nstat
        do 2000,ii1= 1,ii2-1
        iy=ijnd(ii1,ii2)
        t1 = y(iy,jy)
        do 200,j2=jj1+1,nstat
        jx=ijnd(jj1, j2)
        do 200,i2=ii1+1,nstat
        ix=ijnd(ii1, i2)
        t1 = t1 + qq( i2,ii2, j2,jj2)*x(ix,jx)
200     continue
        y(iy,jy) = t1
2000    continue
```

Nevertheless, the loops are far from optimal because they lead to poor data locality for the array x. In the calculation of each element of $y(iy, jy)$, many elements of the array x need to be accessed with large and varying strides.

The possibility of obtaining temporal data locality is suggested by the following observation. All the arrays involved have $\mathcal{O}(nstat^4)$ elements. This is obvious for the array qq, and can be inferred for the arrays x and y from the comment line in each nested loop group. These comment lines indicate the indices on which the elements of x and y indirectly depend via the index arrays ix and jx. Another important observation is that each loop structure has six nested loops, with the consequence that $\mathcal{O}(nstat^6)$ operations are performed. Hence each element is used $\mathcal{O}(nstat^2)$ times, on average. We should try to order the loops in such a way that the elements of both x and y are used at least $\mathcal{O}(nstat)$ times before they are flushed out of cache. In the version above this is not the case for the array x. The complicated structure of the loops, together with their short length, rules out traditional blocking techniques, as the program size and the complexity of such a solution would be unacceptable. Instead, we will try to obtain temporal data locality by reordering the existing loops. This is further complicated by the fact that many start and end values of the inner loops depend on the loop indices of the outer loops.

In the first loop structure, the addresses of the elements of y are independent of $j1$ and $j2$ and the addresses of the elements of x are independent of $jj1$ and $jj2$. This suggests having $j1$ as the innermost loop index followed by $jj1$, $j2$ and $jj2$. Similar arguments apply to the second loop structure. Since y is independent of $i2$ and $j2$ and x independent of $ii2$ and $jj2$, $i2$ is the optimal innermost loop index followed by $ii2$, $j2$ and $jj2$. The new loop orderings are listed below.

```
C y[ ii1 ii2 jj1 jj2 ] x[ ii1 ii2 j1 j2 ]
      do ii2=2,nstat
      do ii1= 1,ii2-1
      ix=ijnd(ii1,ii2)
      iy=ijnd(ii1,ii2)
      do jj2=2,nstat
      do j2=2,nstat
      do jj1= 1,jj2-1
      jy=ijnd(jj1,jj2)
      t1 = y(iy,jy)
      do j1= 1, j2-1
      jx=ijnd( j1, j2)
      t1 = t1 + qq( j1,jj1, j2,jj2)*x(ix,jx)
      t1 = t1 - qq( j1,jj2, j2,jj1)*x(ix,jx)
      enddo
      y(iy,jy) = t1
      enddo
      enddo
      enddo
      enddo
      enddo

C y[ ii1 ii2 jj1 jj2 ] x[ ii1 i2 jj1 j2 ]
      do jj1=1,nstat-1
      do ii1=1,nstat-1
      do jj2=jj1+1,nstat
      jy=ijnd(jj1,jj2)
      do j2=jj1+1,nstat
      jx=ijnd(jj1, j2)
      do ii2=ii1+1,nstat
      iy=ijnd(ii1,ii2)
```

```
t1 = y(iy,jy)
do i2=nstat,ii1+1,-1
ix=ijnd(ii1, i2)
t1 = t1 + qq( i2,ii2, j2,jj2)*x(ix,jx)
enddo
y(iy,jy) = t1
enddo
enddo
enddo
enddo
enddo
```

Let us first discuss the disadvantages present in the new code. The innermost loops are dot products, however the accumulation takes place in the innermost loop, whereas it was done in both the innermost and the second innermost loop in the original version. The effect is a shorter effective DDOT, with the implication of a lower ratio of floating point to load/store operations for the array y. In the original version we had one load/store for $\mathcal{O}(nstat^2)$ updates of y, whereas in the new version this ratio is $\mathcal{O}(nstat)$.

This disadvantage is outweighed by the new temporal data locality of access to x. Since the array elements of x are independent of the second innermost loop, all the $\mathcal{O}(nstat)$ elements that were brought in cache during the first execution of the innermost loop will be reused during the subsequent executions of this loop. If the cache is reasonably large, elements of the array x will be used $\mathcal{O}(nstat)$ times before being flushed out of the cache. For both x and y we now have $\mathcal{O}(nstat)$ uses for one cache miss. If the cache is large enough to hold all the cache lines corresponding to $\mathcal{O}(nstat^2)$ elements of x and y, the ratio of uses to cache misses will be even better, namely $\mathcal{O}(nstat^2)$. In summary thus far, we have eliminated the worst bottleneck of the original loop order, that of the absence of data locality in the memory access of x. The price we had to pay for it, an inferior reuse for y, was worth paying. The program runs five times faster, at 50 Mflops.

Further improvements are possible. Most importantly, unrolling is possible in some loops in order to create several independent operation streams. We have chosen to unroll the second outermost loop by a factor of 4 in both loop structures. In this way, the number of loads for the array qq is reduced. Moreover, the outermost loop could be used for parallelization. An additional 10 to 20 Mflops can be gained by doing transformations of the indices used to address x and y. These transformations require information about the properties of the index arrays. With all these optimizations the loops run at 155 Mflops, i.e., at one-third of the peak performance. This is certainly a respectable result for such a complex sparse matrix-vector multiplication. The optimized code for the first loop structure is listed below.

```
C y[ ii1 ii2 jj1 jj2 ] x[ ii1 ii2 j1 j2 ]
      do ii2=2,nstat

      do ii1= 1,ii2-1-3,4
      ix=ijnd(ii1,ii2)
      iy=ijnd(ii1,ii2)
      do jj2=2,nstat
```

```
do j2=2,nstat
do jj1= 1,jj2-1
jy=ijnd(jj1,jj2)
t1 = y(iy+0,jy)
t2 = y(iy+1,jy)
t3 = y(iy+2,jy)
t4 = y(iy+3,jy)
jx=ijnd( 1, j2)
do j1= 1, j2-1
t1 = t1 + qq( j1,jj1, j2,jj2)*x(ix+0,jx)
t2 = t2 + qq( j1,jj1, j2,jj2)*x(ix+1,jx)
t3 = t3 + qq( j1,jj1, j2,jj2)*x(ix+2,jx)
t4 = t4 + qq( j1,jj1, j2,jj2)*x(ix+3,jx)
t1 = t1 - qq( j1,jj2, j2,jj1)*x(ix+0,jx)
t2 = t2 - qq( j1,jj2, j2,jj1)*x(ix+1,jx)
t3 = t3 - qq( j1,jj2, j2,jj1)*x(ix+2,jx)
t4 = t4 - qq( j1,jj2, j2,jj1)*x(ix+3,jx)
jx=ijnd( j1+1, j2)
enddo
y(iy+0,jy) = t1
y(iy+1,jy) = t2
y(iy+2,jy) = t3
y(iy+3,jy) = t4
enddo
enddo
enddo
enddo


do ii1= ii1,ii2-1
ix=ijnd(ii1,ii2)
iy=ijnd(ii1,ii2)
do jj2=2,nstat
do j2=2,nstat
do jj1= 1,jj2-1
jy=ijnd(jj1,jj2)
t1 = y(iy,jy)
jx=ijnd( 1, j2)
do j1= 1, j2-1
t1 = t1 + qq( j1,jj1, j2,jj2)*x(ix,jx)
t1 = t1 - qq( j1,jj2, j2,jj1)*x(ix,jx)
jx=ijnd( j1+1, j2)
enddo
y(iy,jy) = t1
enddo
enddo
enddo
enddo

enddo
```

For the case of the second loop structure, the unrolling is more complex due to the fact that loop boundaries of inner loops depend on the second outermost loop index. This is left as an exercise for the reader.

Exercise: Unroll the second loop structure in such a way that there are four independent streams. The solution can be found in section A.6 of the appendix.

Table 9.2: *The performance of two CI loops on various machines. The performance of the two original loops listed at the beginning of the section is given for medium and high compiler optimization. For the hand-tuned version, the best compiler options were found by tests.*

	IBM 379	IBM 604	Cray T3E	DEC EV56	DEC EV6
Orig. loops, medium opt.	13	10	13	45	65
Orig. loops, high opt.	15	10	15	47	65
Hand-tuned loops	155	50	70	115	250

Because of the complexity of the loop structures, it is expected that the compilers fail to do such transformations. This is confirmed by the data presented in Table 9.2. In order to do a meaningful comparison, the compiler was provided with all the necessary information to do loop transformations (see section 9.1); i.e., a version of the program was used where the subroutine containing these loops had hard-coded values of the array dimension. We tested three different compiler versions (Version 3, 4 and 5 of XLF) on the IBM Power2 architecture. Hardly any difference was visible between these different versions; in all cases the hand-tuned version, compiled with "-O3" optimization, gave by far the best performance. Allowing loop transformations with the "-qhot" option decreased the performance of the hand-tuned version.

9.4 A two-dimensional wavelet transform

The basic building block for a one-dimensional wavelet transform is a convolution of the type

$$y_i = \sum_{l=-L}^{L} h_l \, x_{i-l}. \tag{9.1}$$

The coefficients h_l are called filter coefficients. Their total number $2L+1$ is small, usually less than a dozen. The number of input data y_i and output data x_i is generally much larger. These two facts already exclude certain program structures. If the innermost loop was the one over the index l, it would be too short to give good performance. In addition, this would result in a bad ratio of floating point operations to loads/stores. Choosing the loop over i as the innermost loop would also result in a bad ratio of floating point operations to loads/stores. In both cases there would be two loads/stores for one addition and one multiplication. The solution to this dilemma is to unroll the loop over l. In this case, the filter coefficients h_l are loop invariant with respect to the loop over i and can be stored in registers. Thus, we have one load only for a combined floating point multiplication-addition, neglecting the single store of the result in y_i. This solution has the additional advantage of allowing us to profit from certain features of the filter. In the case of the interpolating wavelet transform that we are going to consider in this section, the filter coefficients are symmetric and sparse. We are going to take these facts into account for optimization purposes. The downside is that we need to write a new subroutine each time a different set of filters is used. The compiler cannot help in this case either, as this type of information is application dependent and unavailable to the compiler. Based on these considerations, our starting point for the wavelet transform is the following loop structure:

```
      nh=n/2
      do 100,i=0,nh-1
      y(2*i)=x(i)
      y(2*i+1)=x(i+nh)
    & + h1*x(i ) + h1*x(i+1)
    & + h3*x(i-1) + h3*x(i+2)
    & + h5*x(i-2) + h5*x(i+3)
    & + h7*x(i-3) + h7*x(i+4)
    & + h9*x(i-4) + h9*x(i+5)
100   continue
```

The solution found so far still has a serious drawback. We have only one independent stream of operations. However, this is easy to fix. Unrolling the loop over i by a factor of 4, we not only work on y_i, but also on y_{i+1}, y_{i+2}, y_{i+3}, leading to four independent streams. In addition, the ratio of floating point operations to loads is further improved, since many of the array elements x_i are used in all of the four streams. For 40 fused multiply-add instructions we load 17 elements of x and store 8 elements of y. Unrolling the loop over i by a factor larger than 4 would evidently give better ratios, but the current ratio of floating point instructions to load/store instructions is already so advantageous that there is no need for further unrolling. Moreover, unrolling to larger depths may lead to register spilling.

Since unrolling seems so straightforward in this case, we hope that the compiler can do it well. Unfortunately, this is not true. The IBM Fortran compiler xlf version 4.01 does a number of useful optimizations when invoked appropriately ("−O3, −O3 −qhot"). For instance, it realizes that the array element $x(i + 1)$ is equal to the array element $x(i)$ in the next iteration. Therefore it does not reload it, but just copies it in a new register. At the "−O3" level, it also does very aggressive loop unrolling, to a depth of 8 in this case, and succeeds in getting away with it without spilling. Nevertheless, the compiler does not succeed in providing four independent streams. The best compiler-generated code therefore runs at 160 Mflops only for in-cache data on an IBM 590 with a peak speed of 265 Mflops. Unrolling the i loop by hand and assigning scalar variables to all of the array elements leads to a performance of 225 Mflops.

Until now we have only considered a one-dimensional wavelet transform, whereas the goal is a two-dimensional one. In order to do a two-dimensional wavelet transform we need to transform all the rows and all the columns. Denoting indices that refer to nontransformed dimensions by small capital letters and transformed indices by capital letters, we can represent the order of the first transformation as

$$i_1, i_2 \quad \rightarrow \quad I_1, i_2 \quad \rightarrow \quad I_1, I_2.$$

We encounter several problems when implementing a two-dimensional transform in this way. First, we have to write two subroutines, one for the transforms along columns and one for rows. Second, and more important, we cannot get stride 1 in the inner loops in both cases with this scheme. The solution to this problem is known from Fourier transformations [16]. The output of each transformation step is rotated. As we saw in section 6.10, we can get good spatial locality if this rotation is done using blocking. With the index notation defined above, such a scheme can be represented as follows:

$$i_1, i_2 \quad \rightarrow \quad i_2, I_1 \quad \rightarrow \quad I_1, I_2.$$

Another problem that was ignored in the one-dimensional wavelet transform is related to the boundary conditions in the problem. Let's consider the widely used case of periodic boundary conditions. This means that the subscript $(i - l)$ of the input data x in (9.1) has to be wrapped around once it is out of bounds. If the allowed range of values for the index of the input data is the interval $[0, n - 1]$, then a value of $n + 2$ has to be mapped back to 2. This mapping can be done by either using the modulus function or employing if statements. Both variants are expensive. If the mapped index values were precalculated once and for all, we would double the number of loads and introduce indirectly indexed data structures. All of these possibilities would lead to a considerable slowdown and prevent using the index to be transformed as the index of the innermost loop. Fortunately, in the case of the two-dimensional transform, there is an easy solution to this dilemma. Since we have to do multiple transformations, we can use the index that runs over all of the multiple data sets as the index of the innermost loop. Thus, we get the following loop structure:

```
        nh=n/2
c transform loop
        do 100,i=0,nh-1
          ii00=i
          iim1=mod(i-1+nh,nh)
          iim2=mod(i-2+nh,nh)
          iim3=mod(i-3+nh,nh)
          iim4=mod(i-4+nh,nh)
          iip1=mod(i+1,nh)
          iip2=mod(i+2,nh)
          iip3=mod(i+3,nh)
          iip4=mod(i+4,nh)
          iip5=mod(i+5,nh)
c loop over all multiple data sets
          do 200,j=1,m
          y(j,2*i)=x(ii00,j)
          y(j,2*i+1)=x(ii00+nh,j)
     &      + h1*x(ii00,j) + h1*x(iip1,j)
     &      + h3*x(iim1,j) + h3*x(iip2,j)
     &      + h5*x(iim2,j) + h5*x(iip3,j)
     &      + h7*x(iim3,j) + h7*x(iip4,j)
     &      + h9*x(iim4,j) + h9*x(iip5,j)
200     continue
100     continue
```

Applying this loop structure twice leads to a two-dimensional transform. Since we now have a nonunit stride access of x, it follows from the discussion in section 6.10

Table 9.3: *Performance results (in Mflops) for a two-dimensional wavelet transform*

	IBM 590		ORIGIN 2000	
	Hand-tuned	Best compiler	Hand-tuned	Best compiler
In cache	210	125	200	130
Out of cache	150	20	130	40

that we have to block this loop structure if the data set is too large to fit in cache. Unfortunately, we cannot rely on the compiler for blocking. Even after trying many combinations of compiler options for aggressive optimization, we were not able to produce efficient blocked code. This applies to both the IBM compiler xlf version 4.02 and to the SGI compiler f77 version MIPSpro_7.2.1. Most likely, similar problems are found with the compilers of other vendors too.

In the final hand-optimized version, the loop over i was unrolled by a factor of 4, the loop over j was blocked and all array elements were assigned to scalar variables. In addition, the calculation of the wrapped-around indices was done by if statements, instead of the slightly more expensive modulus function. The schematic loop structure is shown below.

```
       dimension x(n1+b1,n2+b2),y(n1+b1,n2+b2)

       . . . . . . . . . . . . . . .

       do 2000,jj=1,m,lot
       j0=jj
       j1=min(jj+lot-1,m)

       do 100,i=0,nh-4,4

       . . . . . . . . . . . . . . .

       do 200,j=j0,j1

       . . . . . . . . . . . . . . .

200    continue
100    continue
2000   continue
```

The results for this hand-optimized routine and the best compiler effort are shown in Table 9.3. The reason for the speedup in the case of in-cache data is that there are four independent streams in the hand-optimized version. The deviation from peak speed (265 Mflops on the 590) comes from the substantial loop overheads for these complicated loops. The speedup for out of cache data is mainly due to blocking. The blocking parameter *lot* and the optimal leading dimension $n1+b1, n2+b2$ were determined by the routine "cache_par" of section 6.7. For fairness, the tests with the compiler-optimized code were done with the same optimal leading dimensions.

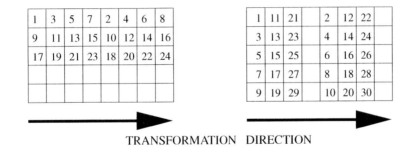

TRANSFORMATION DIRECTION

Figure 9.1: *The data access pattern for a multiple FFT, where five data sets of length 8 are transformed. A Fortran column major ordering is assumed. On the left, the inner loop is over a single FFT sweep, resulting in a nonlocal data access pattern. On the right, the inner loop runs over the five data sets, leading to good spatial data locality.*

9.5 A three-dimensional fast Fourier transform

The main difficulty when optimizing fast Fourier transforms (FFTs) [29] is related to the highly nonlocal data access pattern. Therefore, in this case study we will concentrate only on this point and neglect the less important aspect of the floating point operation optimization [15].

A Fourier transformation consists of a series of sweeps. The number of sweeps depends on the number of prime factors in which the length of the data set can be factored. If the length n of the data set is a power of 2, there are $\log_2(n)$ sweeps. In the first sweep, data that are $n/2$ words apart are accessed; in the next sweep, data that are $n/4$ words apart; and so on, all the way to the final sweep where neighboring data are accessed. If the data set does not fit in cache, this data access pattern lacks spatial locality, particularly in the first few sweeps, leading to serious performance degradation on RISC machines. Even if the data fit in cache, the calculation of the addresses is relatively complicated and slow. On vector machines, memory access problems arise as well, since the same memory banks will be repeatedly accessed.

In many scientific applications, three-dimensional FFTs are needed instead of one-dimensional FFTs. Three-dimensional FFTs require consecutive transformations of all the data along the three axes. The memory access problem can be alleviated by constructing the three-dimensional FFTs from multiple FFTs. In a multiple FFT, the loop that runs over all the multiple data sets to be transformed should be the innermost loop. As shown in Figure 9.1, stride 1 can be obtained in the innermost loop.

We will now discuss efficient implementations of three-dimensional FFTs, not only on RISC machines, as we did in the other case studies, but also on vector and parallel machines. Since the implementation on vector machines is the most elegant, we will start with the vector machines and then modify the scheme to adapt it to the other architectures. As in our discussion of wavelet transforms, we will denote nontransformed dimensions by $i1, i2, i3$ and their transformed analogs by $I1, I2, I3$.

9.5.1   Vector machines

Optimal speed can be obtained on a vector machine if the vectorizable inner loop is long and no memory bank conflicts are present. This can be obtained easily in a multiple FFT. Starting with our initial data set

$$i1, i2, i3$$

we first transform along the last dimension $i3$. To obtain the longest possible inner loop length, we merge the first two dimensions into a single one:

$$i1 \times i2, i3.$$

Frequently, the number of data along the first and second dimensions n_1 and n_2 is a multiple of a power of 2. In this case we have a memory bank conflict. Let us assume that we are at a certain stage of a sweep where we work on the data associated with $i_3 = 1$ and $i_3 = 9$. The data items $i1, i2, 1$ and $i1, i2, 9$ will be separated by $8 * n_1 * n_2$ words. If $8 * n1 * n2$ is a multiple of the number of memory banks—a likely occurrence as the number of memory banks typically is between 128 and 1024—then both data items $i1, i2, 1$ and $i1, i2, 9$ will be located in the same memory bank. Since the same memory bank has to recover during the refresh time before it can service a second memory access, a substantially reduced memory bandwidth will result. This problem can be overcome by introducing effective dimensions nd_1 and nd_2 that are not multiples of powers of 2. If $n_1 = 64$, then a good choice for nd_1 is 65. By using this trick, the data items are now separated by $8 * nd_1 * nd_2$ words and will not reside in the same memory bank. It is clear that this problem is only relevant to transform lengths that are powers of 2. For a nonpower of 2 FFT, say of size $81 \times 81 \times 81$, the effective dimensions nd_1, nd_2, nd_3 can be equal to the physical transform lengths n_1, n_2, n_3. Choosing slightly larger effective dimensions will cause a small extra overhead. Instead of transforming $n_1 * n_2$ data sets, we now have to transform $nd_1 * n_2$ data sets. The penalty for this extra overhead is very small compared to the performance degradation we would incur due to repeated hits of the same memory bank.

On the last sweep of the multiple FFT, we combine it with a transposition of the data set to obtain

$$I3, i1 \times i2 \to I3, i1, i2.$$

This transposition implies a nonunit stride for the output array. On most vector machines, nonunit stride is just as fast as unit stride as long as there are no problems with the memory bank access. To avoid such problems, we introduce a dimension nd_3 that is not a power of 2. We then repeat exactly the same procedure two more times to get

$$I2, I3, i1$$

and, finally,

$$I1, I2, I3.$$

Table 9.4: *Performance of three-dimensional FFTs on a Cray C90 vector computer. The rotation technique "ROT" is compared with the CCFFT3D routine from the Cray library.*

Dimension	32	64	100	125	128
CCFFT3D	83	240	350	380	470
ROT	760	810	560	580	780

In this symbolic notation we have suppressed the fact that the first two indices are merged in both steps to obtain long inner loop lengths, just as they were in the first step.

By using this technique, substantial speed can be obtained on vector machines. Typically more than half of the peak speed is obtained, which can be as high as 1 Gigaflops on the fastest vector machines. Even higher performance can be obtained on modestly parallel vector computer configurations. Table 9.4 shows some performance measurements on a Cray C90 with this algorithm together with the performance of the CCFFT3D routines from the Cray library. Apparently, the data management in the Cray routine is not optimal. Because of the long inner loop lengths, our routine is substantially faster for small data sets.

9.5.2 RISC machines

On RISC architectures a slight modification of the scheme designed for vector machines leads to good performance. We start again with our data set

$$i1, i2, i3$$

and first transform along the last dimension $i3$. Blocking is necessary in order to obtain temporal data locality across different sweeps. Therefore, we first merge the first two indices, and afterwards we split them up in a different way:

$$i1, i2, i3 \rightarrow i1 \times i2, i3 \rightarrow j \times k, i3 \rightarrow j, k, i3.$$

j runs from 1 to lot and k from 1 to $nd_2 * nd_3/lot$. We choose lot such that $nd_3 * lot$ words fit in cache. To avoid cache thrashing we choose the effective dimensions nd_1, nd_2 and nd_3 appropriately, as discussed before. We then do all the FFT sweeps for lot multiple transforms, having all the data in cache after the first sweep. The last sweep is combined with a data transposition. We repeat this series of sweeps for all of the $nd_2 * nd_3/lot$ bunches of lot multiple transforms to obtain

$$I3, i1, i2.$$

Repeating the whole procedure two more times leads to the final result.

While the whole procedure is very similar to the one for vector machines, there are two differences. On the vector machine, we tried to get the longest possible inner loop length by taking the product of the first two indices. On RISC, we split

Table 9.5: *Performance of a 128^3 three-dimensional FFT on the IBM Power2 (120 Mhz), Compaq/DEC EV56 (467 Mhz), Compaq EV6/DEC (500 Mhz) and SGI R10000 (195 Mhz). The rotation technique "ROT" described in this chapter is compared with the library of FFT routines "FFTW" from http://www.fftw.org/.*

Machine	IBM Power2	DEC EV56	DEC EV6	SGI R10000
FFTW	35	140		65
ROT	210	150	400	140

the inner loop into bunches of size *lot* to use the cache effectively. To avoid cache thrashing, the effective dimensions have to be different from the physical dimensions on both architectures, but the rules for their determination are different.

Even on a RISC machine it is important to have reasonably long inner loop lengths. If the cache size is very small, the length of the inner loop *lot* may be too small to obtain high speed. Large cache sizes are therefore important for high performance with three-dimensional FFTs. Depending on the cache size and on the memory bandwidth, the performance can vary considerably. On an IBM 590 with a rather large cache, the FFT runs at 110 Mflops out of a peak speed of 266, whereas on a Cray T3E processor (Compaq Alpha), with a small L1 cache, the code runs at 95 Mflops for a peak speed of 800 Mflops. The speeds obtained on several recent processors with the technique described before are shown in Table 9.5.

9.5.3   Parallel machines

In this section we describe the organization of the data traffic for a three-dimensional FFT on a parallel computer. In addition to striving to achieve efficiency, two other considerations will guide us. We would like to reuse the serial multiple FFT routines developed for the RISC and vector machines and would also like to have the flexibility to easily construct higher multidimensional cases. We start again with the data set

$$i1, i2, i3.$$

The first thing we have to decide is how to distribute the initial data among the processors. We choose to distribute the last index $i3$. For example, assuming that we want to do a $64 \times 64 \times 64$ transform on 8 processors, the first processor will own all of the data with $i3 = 1, \ldots, 8$, the second processor, all of the data with $i3 = 9, \ldots, 16$, and so on. This data distribution implies that $n3$ is a multiple of the number of processors. If that is not the case, we have to introduce an effective dimension md_3 that is such a multiple. The minor inefficiency related to the fact that the last processor has to transform all of the useless padded data in the buffer region between n_3 and md_3 is unavoidable. Since our FFT algorithm will be based on data transpositions, it turns out that the other two effective dimensions md_1 and md_2 need to be multiples of the number of processors as well. In our symbolic notation, we split up the last index into two indices

$$i1, i2, i3 \rightarrow i1, i2, j3, jp3,$$

where $jp3$ runs over all the $nproc$ processors and $j3 = 1, \ldots, md_3/nproc$. Then, we do a transformation along the $i2$ axis for all of the two-dimensional data sets $i1, i2$. We use exactly the same procedure that we presented for RISC machines, which means that the data are transposed on the last sweep. Since there are $md_3/nproc$ two-dimensional data sets, we have to do $md_3/nproc$ such transforms. The final result is

$$I2, i1, j3, jp3. \tag{9.2}$$

Next, we split up the first index $i1$ into $jp1$ and $j1$, such that $jp1 = 1, \ldots, nproc$ and $j1 = 1, \ldots, md_1/nproc$:

$$I2, j1, jp1, j3, jp3,$$

and reorder the data set

$$I2, j1, j3, jp1, jp3.$$

This reordering is cache friendly, since it can be done with an inner loop where all array accesses have stride 1. Next, we do a data transposition among the processors using the MPI_ALLTOALL routine. In our symbolic notation, this has the effect of switching the last two indices:

$$I2, j1, j3, jp3, jp1.$$

Finally, we do another cache-friendly reordering to obtain

$$I2, j3, jp3, j1, jp1,$$

which is equal to

$$I2, i3, j1, jp1.$$

This has the same structure as our initial data set (9.2), up to a shift in all indices. Repeating exactly the same series of steps two more times, we transform along the $i3$ and $i1$ axes to complete the three-dimensional FFT.

Several additional data reshuffling steps, both on processor and interprocessor with the MPI routine, are required compared to the single processor case. The single processor data reordering steps introduce a substantial overhead. While a serial two-dimensional FFT based on this kernel runs at 95 Mflops on a T3E processor, the parallel version reaches just half this speed per processor. Figure 9.2 shows the performance of different FFTs on the CRAY T3E, the SGI Origin 2000 and IBM SP2. On the Cray, we compare an implementation based on the method outlined here with Cray's "PCCFFT3D" library routine. Very good speedups are obtained with both routines on the Cray. Nevertheless, it has to be noted that a very large number of T3E processors are needed to reach the performance of a single node vector processor. On the Origin 2000 it is impossible to obtain high performance on any number of processors. FFTs are a particularly difficult task for parallel machines since the ratio of floating point operations to interprocessor communication is small. Low latency, together with a high bisectional bandwidth, are therefore very important. The Cray T3E is appropriate from this point of view.

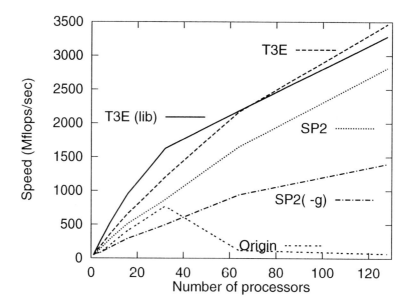

Figure 9.2: *The parallel performance of a 128^3 FFT on the Cray T3E, IBM SP2 and SGI Origin2000. On the Cray we show the performance of both our implementation and the PCCFFT3D library, denoted by "lib." Two results are also shown for the IBM. With the "$-g$" option, all four processors in the SMP node are used; without it only one processor per node is utilized. The counterintuitive result, that the performance is better only if one processor per node is used, is related to its better bisectional bandwidth, as described in Figure 2.10. The timings on the Origin2000 were characterized by large fluctuations. The best timing data is plotted.*

Exercise: Show that one can construct a three-dimensional FFT with only two MPI_ALLTOALL interprocessor communication steps instead of the three steps in the method described above. The disadvantage of this approach is that the coding effort is higher since the full three-dimensional FFT is no longer a thrice repeated sequence of identical steps. Test by how much you can outperform the Cray PCCFFT3D routine with this approach. For the basic multiple FFTs use the Cray MLTFFT routine or any other efficient multiple FFT.

9.6   Multigrid methods on parallel machines

Multigrid methods [10] are a standard family of methods for the solution of elliptic partial differential equations (PDEs). The multigrid method smooths the different wavelengths found in these equations on grids of different resolutions, leading to a highly efficient scheme. In the two-dimensional case, each resolution level k has 4^k grid points (Figure 9.3); in the three-dimensional case, 8^k grid points. During the solution process grid levels are successively visited. Different multigrid schemes relate to the order in which grid levels are traversed. One standard recipe is the "V-

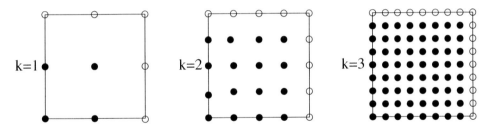

Figure 9.3: *Three different grid levels (k = 1, k = 2 and k = 3) used in a two-dimensional multigrid scheme. Since periodic boundary conditions are implied, the points on the upper left edges, denoted by open circles, have the same values as the points on the lower left edges.*

cycle," in which the grid levels are traversed from the finest to the coarsest and back up to the finest level. Regardless of the multigrid scheme utilized, a few smoothing steps are done on each grid, using simple iterative methods such as the Gauss–Seidel relaxation. The transfer of error approximation from a coarse to a finer grid is done using a restriction operator, while the inverse transfer is accomplished using an interpolation operator. By repeating the cycle several times, the solution of the partial differential equation on the finest grid can be determined with any desired accuracy.

Communication requirements in parallel implementations of multigrid methods are significant, being determined by the need to exchange boundary information among the subdomains distributed across processors. Moreover, surface-to-volume effects are very important in multigrid, as this ratio is very different when traversing the grid levels. This poses a serious efficiency dilemma, suggesting the need for varying the number of active processors during the computation. A detailed analysis of both aspects follows. We note here that the initial distribution of data has to be done based on the principle described in section 8.5. The subdomains assigned to each processors have to be as close as possible to a square in two dimensions or a cube in three dimensions for the Cartesian grids discussed here.

- *Parallel optimization issues related to surface-to-volume effects:* A straight-forward implementation would involve marching through all grid levels using the full processor configuration. Given the fact that the number of grid points becomes very small on the coarsest level, this solution would lead to a very poor surface-to-volume ratio on the coarse grids. The processors would be involved in numerous and small message communications while computing on a very small number of grid points. The inefficiency of such an implementation is obvious.

  We can substantially improve the performance by varying the number of processors utilized with the grid level. This "dynamic" processor allocation introduces additional complications due to the need for data redistribution each time the processor configuration changes. Several methods to achieve the desired effect of communication optimization are possible.

0	4	8	12
1	5	9	13
2	6	10	14
3	7	11	15

0/4/ 1/5	8/12/ 9/13
2/6/ 3/7	10/14/ 11/15

Figure 9.4: *At very coarse levels the number of processors is no longer reduced, but work is duplicated. On levels below a certain threshold, all the processors (16 in this example) work on their own domain. On levels above, groups of 4 processor do identical calculations.*

One method involves the abrupt reduction in the number of processors beyond a "threshold" grid level. Typically, this involves the reduction of the number of processors to a single one, as soon as the grid becomes coarse enough. If we have N_{fine} grid points on the fine grid, the total number of grid points on all of the coarse grid levels is given by $N_{fine}(\frac{1}{8} + \frac{1}{64} + \cdots) = N_{fine}\frac{1}{7}$. Hence $\frac{7}{8}$ of the total workload has to be done on the finest grid and good performance can be obtained on a small number of processors.

Exercise: What maximum speedup does Amdahl's law predict for the above-outlined method on a four-processor machine?

In a second procedure, the number of processors is gradually reduced beyond the threshold grid level. After the finest grid levels have been visited, we begin reducing the number of processors by redistributing the data so that the surface-to-volume remains constant. The procedure is reversed when moving up towards the finest grid levels. This method leads to better performance than the first one, with the downside that the complexity of the code increases.

A third alternative, which can be applied in conjunction with the first or the second, involves having the idle processors duplicate the computation so that the cost of data redistribution on the up side of the cycle is eliminated (in scenario 1) or reduced (in scenario 2). This variant is schematically shown in Figure 9.4 for a two-dimensional grid.

In summary, in the best possible implementation we distinguish three different regimes. On the finest grids, all available processors are used; beyond a threshold grid level, the number of active processors is gradually reduced; and for the coarsest grid levels, the number of active processors is fixed, but the work is replicated on all idling processors.

- *How to organize the communication for the smoothing step on each level:* This discussion applies not only to multigrid methods, but to any grid-based method using rectangular stencils. We consider the problem of updating each

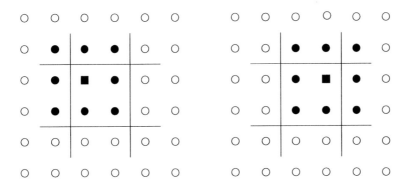

Figure 9.5: *A grid partitioning where four grid points (shown by circles) are associated with one processor. On the left, all the points needed to update the upper left grid point (denoted by a square) are shown by black circles. Similarly on the right, for the upper right grid point. Note that this stencil is more complicated than the one shown in Figure 8.3.*

grid point using operations that require the values on a stencil as shown in Figure 9.5. In multigrid, such an operation has to be done for the smoothing step performed on each grid level. A straightforward solution would be the following. Any processor sends all its edge points to the upper, lower, right and left processors and all its corner points to the four processors along the diagonals. We would have to send 8 messages of two different types. In the three-dimensional case the situation is even more complicated. We have to distinguish between corners, edges and faces, resulting in three different message types for a total of 26 messages. Trying to send all these messages at the same time would result in a backlog of messages, since messages are sent and/or received one at a time on all the parallel computers mentioned in this book. In addition, sending many short messages involves high latency costs.

Fortunately, the communication step can be organized in a better way. In the two-dimensional case, we subdivide this communication step into four phases where all the processors send edge points downward, upward, to the right and, finally, to the left. In the third and fourth phases, the processors send not only their own edge points, but a prolongated edge that contains the points they received in the two previous phases from other processors. In this way, the corner point that has to be sent along the diagonal will arrive at its destination processor not directly but via an intermediate processor. The scheme is explained in detail in Figure 9.6. In the two-dimensional case this communication scheme reduces the number of messages per processor from 8 to 4. In the three-dimensional case the saving is even larger: 6 messages instead of 26.

The scheme for optimization of the smoothing step, together with the strategies proposed for communication optimization due to surface-to-volume variation, lead

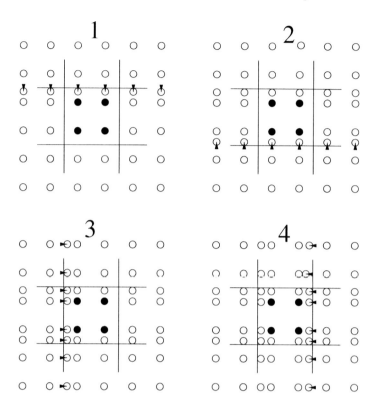

Figure 9.6: *The four phases of the communication step in the multigrid smoothing step. We concentrate our attention on the processor in the middle that holds the four grid points denoted by black dots. In the first phase all processors send their edge points downward; in the second phase, upward. After these two phases, the left and right processors hold a prolongated edge that contains not only their original edge points, but also the corner points that were originally on the upper/lower left/right processor. In the third and fourth phases, where the messages are exchanged to the left and to the right, these prolongated edges are sent to the processor in the middle, which then has all the data points needed for the smoothing step.*

to good performance and scalability for parallel multigrid implementations. Of course, the key is in tuning these strategies for the specific PDEs, multigrid scheme and parallel architecture utilized.

A benchmark three-dimensional multigrid problem is contained in the NAS Parallel Benchmarks suite, to be discussed in the following section. This benchmark requires the solution of the Poisson equation utilizing a V-cycle multigrid scheme on $256 \times 256 \times 256$ grid points on the finest grid level. The solution adopted by IBM is described in [2] and is very similar to the optimal method presented in this chapter. Some performance results are presented in Table 9.6.

Table 9.6: *Performance in Mflops of the NAS multigrid benchmark on the Cray T3E, IBM SP2 and SGI Origin2000 with various numbers of processors.*

T3E: 8	T3E: 64	SP2: 1	SP2: 64	Origin: 1	Origin: 64
769	4865	82	3313	78	3972

9.7 A real-world electronic structure code

In the last case study we will present a widely used electronic structure code [19] developed by Hutter and coworkers. In contrast to the previous case studies, we are expanding the scope from one or several subroutines to a full-blown real-world code designed to solve large-scale applications in academic and industrial environments. The code comprises some 100,000 lines and runs on most current computers ranging from workstations to vector computers and massively parallel computers. Portability has been achieved by using standard libraries such as BLAS, LAPACK and the MPI message library. The program allows the simulation of any condensed matter composed of electrons and nuclei, such as atoms, molecules, solids and liquids. The quantum mechanical equations for the electrons are solved using the density-functional approximation (http://www.nobel.se/chemistry/laureates/1998). The nuclei are treated as classical particles. The program can do static and dynamic electronic structure calculations. In dynamic simulations, the nuclei move under the influence of the forces exerted by the electrons. Given this functionality, the user can either do geometry optimization of molecules and solids or molecular dynamics simulations. Depending on the kind of atoms contained in the system, the maximum system size that can be treated on a large-scale parallel machine varies between 50 and 500 atoms. Plane waves are used as the basis set for the expansion of the electron wave-function, as well as for other quantities.

Typical applications for electronic structure programs of this type are the design of new materials and drugs, the improvement of the efficiency of chemical reactions and the prediction of the behavior of matter under extreme conditions, such as in stars or explosions. The elucidation of such problems by computer simulation is frequently faster and cheaper than the traditional experimental investigation in the laboratory. In addition, quantities are accessible that cannot be measured experimentally.

In spite of the length of the program, the CPU-intensive parts are rather small and well defined. A profiling of the codes shows that, for small molecules, the three-dimensional FFT takes most of the CPU time (90%). The FFTs are needed to switch back and forth between the real space and Fourier representations needed at various stages of the calculation. The serial and parallel optimization of FFTs was done along the lines discussed in section 9.5. There we saw that FFTs of moderate size do not scale very well to a very large number of processors. To improve this scaling, the physical structure of the problem can be exploited in CPMD. Since the FFTs have to be done on all the individual electron orbitals, parallelization is done with respect to these orbitals too. This twofold parallelization strategy

Table 9.7: *Performance numbers on the Cray T3E, on up to 64 processors for a small atomic system consisting of 64 silicon atoms. The performance numbers in this and the following table were kindly provided to us by Juerg Hutter from the University of Zürich.*

NCPU	1	2	4	8	16	32	64
Speedup	1	1.92	3.68	7.11	12.5	20.7	45.3
Mflops	98	188	360	697	1225	2030	4440

Table 9.8: *Performance numbers on the Cray T3E for a system of 32 water molecules. Because of memory requirements, the smallest possible configuration consists of eight processors.*

NCPU	8	16	32	64	128	256
Speedup	1	1.92	3.75	6.07	10.8	22.7

represents an optimal compromise between communication cost and load balancing considerations. Good speedups can be obtained for large atomic systems on large number of processors, such as 512. The bottleneck for the FFT performance in CPMD on RISC-based parallel machines is the serial performance, limited by the memory bandwidth, as described in section 9.5. For systems containing a large number of atoms, the nonlocal component of the pseudopotential becomes a major component (up to half) of the CPU time. Pseudopotentials eliminate the chemically inert core electrons that cannot be represented efficiently in a plane wave basis. The numerical treatment of the nonlocal pseudopotential involves matrix times matrix multiplications. Vendor-optimized BLAS routines are used for these operations. These routines, tuned in a manner similar to that described in section 9.1, achieve a significant fraction of the serial peak speed. The parallelization of the pseudopotential calculations is done by distributing the Fourier space grid among the different processors as described in section 8.5, while replicating the overlap matrices. This leads to nearly perfect load balancing and an advantageous ratio of computation to communication. Consequently, very good speedups can be obtained in this part of the code. Linear algebra routines from parallel mathematical libraries were not used because of the inflexibility of the data structures that they require. The overall and parallel performances under strong scalability tests in two different calculations are shown in Tables 9.7 and 9.8.

These performance numbers demonstrate that it is possible to achieve high performance on massively parallel machines in realistic applications using the state-of-the-art optimization techniques described in this book.

Chapter 10

Benchmarks

In this chapter a sketch of the benchmarking arena is attempted and some widely utilized benchmarks will be presented. Given the extent of this activity, at both a scientific and a technical level, but also related to computer procurement, we cannot render justice to it in a short section. We refer the reader to comprehensive books on performance analysis and benchmarking such as [11] and [6].

Benchmarks can be classified according to the complexity of the measurement and of the code on which they are based. Low-level benchmarks aim at providing data for simple, low-level, architectural parameters such as the latency and the bandwidth of the network. "Parkbench" (http://www.netlib.org/parkbench/), for example, contains a collection of such benchmarks. Moving upwards in the hierarchy, we distinguish kernel benchmarks, measuring performance of certain loop constructs or compiler optimizations of simple code fragments. The "Livermore loops" (http://www.llnl.gov/asci_benchmarks/asci/limited/lfk/asci_lfk.html) are representative of such benchmarks. Higher up in the hierarchy are benchmarks for certain well-defined mathematical algorithms such as the solution of linear systems, simple multigrid schemes, etc. LINPACK and the NAS parallel benchmarks are important examples in this category. At the highest level, benchmarks for entire applications have been proposed. However, due to the complexity of the analysis and optimization and the high number of degrees of freedom in interpreting benchmarks at this level, full application benchmarks are not nearly as widely utilized as the others.

Benchmarks are prescribed in various forms. Some of the higher level benchmarks are aimed at assessing the best level of performance that can be achieved on a machine. They specify only the mathematical problem that needs to be solved and leave complete freedom to all the implementation details. The NAS parallel benchmarks (http://www.nas.nasa.gov/Software/NPB) are the most representative suite of pencil-and-paper defined benchmarks. Other benchmarks provide source code that must not be modified, relying entirely on the compiler for optimizations.

One of the best known of the floating point benchmarks is the LINPACK benchmark (http://www.netlib/org/). One class of this benchmark is aimed at single processors and SMPs, and another class at massively parallel machines. In each

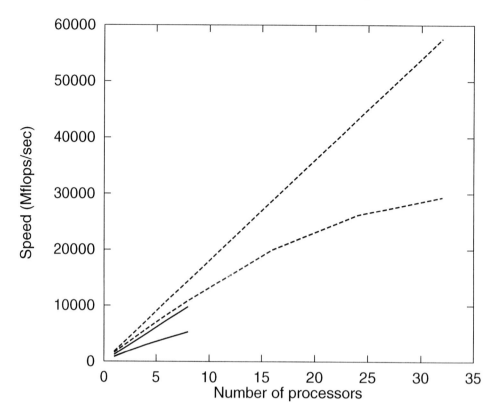

Figure 10.1: *The theoretical peak speed and the actual LINPACK 1000 speed on a vector SMP and RISC SMP. The results are shown for the Cray T90 (dashed line) and the Compaq/DEC EV6 based SMP (solid line). These two SMPs were the fastest vector and RISC SMP in the LINPACK benchmark of July 1999, from where the data are taken.*

class, two categories are present. In the first category, a linear system of equations of dimension 100 × 100 is solved without any hand optimization. Only compiler optimization is allowed. In the second category, the system of equations is of dimension 1000 × 1000 and hand optimizations are allowed as long as they do not significantly reduce the accuracy of the result. A look at the single processor class shows that vector processors are still ahead of the RISC processors in this type of calculation. The highest performance is obtained on shared memory vector systems. An examination of the data for this type of architecture reveals some of the performance problems of SMPs already mentioned in this book. For the 100 × 100 category, in most cases, it is impossible to get reasonable speedup on larger processor configurations. Consequently, vendors provide data for only a very small configuration, i.e., of two or at most four processors. Even in the 1000 × 1000 case the speedups are not very good, as shown in Figure 10.1.

It is also interesting to look at the difference in performance of the 100 × 100 and 1000 × 1000 categories on single RISC processors. The performance in the first category is typically lower by a factor of 2 to 3. Since loop lengths of the order of 100 are sufficient for good performance on RISC machines, this difference is mainly due to hand optimization versus compiler optimization. This big difference exists in spite of the enormous effort by vendors attempting to improve compiler technology. Moreover, folklore abounds with stories of compilers recognizing the LINPACK loops and optimizing them "under the hood."

In a special LINPACK class for massively parallel machines, the problem size is allowed to vary. Weak scalability is thus tested instead of strong scalability. All of the massively parallel computers in this class are RISC based. Performance in excess of a Teraflop for matrices of order 100,000 were obtained. The massively parallel machines in these tests are unique architectures consisting of several thousand processors linked by a high-performance network. It is very important to note that the massively parallel LINPACK benchmark is a relatively easy problem. Since the number of floating point operations grows cubically with the linear system size, whereas the communication grows only quadratically, the problem necessarily becomes coarse-grained for large enough systems. In practice, such dense systems of equations occur very rarely and, instead, iterative algorithms that scale linearly with respect to the problem size and involve sparse matrices are usually utilized. In such algorithms, the scaling of the problem would look completely different from LINPACK. This situation is typical for the pitfalls in utilizing kernel benchmarks in predicting performance in a context different from the very specific goal of the benchmark.

A parallel benchmark suite that is far more realistic than the parallel LINPACK is the NAS Parallel benchmark. It contains several real-life algorithms and pseudo-applications of fixed problem size, specified in a pencil-and-paper form. Given the fixed problem size, it therefore tests strong scalability. Because of this difference, together with the much more stringent communication requirements of most of the algorithms in the NAS suite, the performance of the massively parallel machines looks less attractive. The speedup degrades considerably for most of the kernels for configurations of the order of a few hundred processors or less, depending on the performance of the interprocessor communication. Some specific data was provided in the section on multigrid, section 9.6. The best performance that can be obtained exceeds that of a single vector processor by only one order of magnitude, roughly. The highest absolute performance in the NAS benchmarks are obtained on shared memory vector processors.

The SPEC benchmark is another widely accepted benchmark (http://www.specbench.org). SPEC is based on programs of fixed size. Results are not reported in Mflops, but in "Specs." SPEC contains both single processor and SMP RISC benchmarks, but no vector machines. Since the codes are more complex, they probably reflect reality better than LINPACK. Hand optimization is not allowed, hence the compiler has an important role to play. It is interesting to see how widely the best compiler options vary across machines. They range through all levels of optimization, from "−O2" to "−O5," and include an incredible collection of obscure compiler options.

Finally, some workload-specific benchmarks have been proposed, attempting to analyze and predict the performance of a suite of compact applications representa-

Table 10.1: *Price/performance figures (Mflops/($1000)) for recent Gordon Bell Award winners in the price/performance category, for the years 1994–1997. Data can be found at http://www.computer.org/ and http://www.supercomp.org/*

Year	1994	1995	1996	1997
Price/performance ratio	3.0	3.6	6.3	11

tive of a specific workload. The ASCI compact application suite is an example of this type of benchmark. The codes in these benchmarks are representative of the scientific computations performed on Teraflop-scale parallel systems at several national laboratories in the United States. A methodology for performance modeling and prediction for applications related to these applications is presented in [18].

All the discussion of performance in this book has neglected one important aspect of daily life, namely, the cost of computing. In taking this aspect into account, the performance landscape may look quite different. As an example, high-speed memories, divided among a large number of banks, may look much less attractive. The progress made in recent years in that respect is quite astonishing. A good indicator of the price/performance evolution is the Gordon Bell Award. One Gordon Bell Award category is for a scientific application that achieves the best price/performance number on a parallel machine. The numbers for some recent years are shown in Table 10.1.

In spite of the numerous benchmarks available, it cannot be taken for granted that any of them will accurately predict the performance of a particular user program. The most specific benchmark is therefore one's own suite of most heavily used programs.

Appendix

For online information about obtaining the programs listed in this appendix, please
see this book's feature page on SIAM's website at http://www.siam.org/books/set12/

A.1   Timing routine for BLAS library

```
C  Speed of different level BLAS routines. A simple matrix times matrix
C  multiplication is done directly and by decomposing it into nd matrix
C  times vector multiplications or nd**2 scalar products.

       program blaslevels

       implicit real*8 (a-h,o-z)
       parameter(nd=1000)
       dimension a(nd,nd),b(nd,nd),c(nd,nd)

       do 15,j=1,nd
       do 15,i=1,nd
       a(i,j)=1.d0
       b(i,j)=2.d0
       c(i,j)=3.d0
15     continue

c level 3:
       t1=mclock()*1.d-2
         call DGEMM('N','N',nd,nd,nd,1.d0,a,nd,b,nd,0.d0,c,nd)
       t2=mclock()*1.d-2
       time_sec=(t2-t1)
       speed_Mflops=(2*nd**3/time_sec)*1.d-6
       cycle=time_sec*cyclehertz/(2*nd**3)
       write(6,*) 'DGEMM RESULTS --------------'
       write(6,*) 'SPEED (MFLOPS)',speed_Mflops

c level 2:
       t1=mclock()*1.d-2
       do i=1,nd
```

```
      call DGEMV('N',nd,nd,1.d0,a,nd,b(1,i),1,0.d0,c(1,i),1)
      enddo
      t2=mclock()*1.d-2
      time_sec=(t2-t1)
      speed_Mflops=(2*nd**3/time_sec)*1.d-6
      cycle=time_sec*cyclehertz/(2*nd**3)
      write(6,*) 'DGEMV RESULTS --------------'
      write(6,*) 'SPEED (MFLOPS)',speed_Mflops

c level 1:
      t1=mclock()*1.d-2
      do j=1,nd
      do i=1,nd
        c(i,j)=DDOT(nd,a(1,i),1,b(1,j),1)
      enddo
      enddo
      t2=mclock()*1.d-2
      time_sec=(t2-t1)
      speed_Mflops=(2*nd**3/time_sec)*1.d-6
      cycle=time_sec*cyclehertz/(2*nd**3)
      write(6,*) 'DDOT RESULTS --------------'
      write(6,*) 'SPEED (MFLOPS)',speed_Mflops

      end
```

A.2   MPI timing routine

```
      subroutine timing(category,action,nflop,iproc,nproc)
c subroutine for performance analysis of parallel MPI programs
c possible actions are:
c     'INI' to initialize all the counters at the beginning of program
c     'STR' to (re)start accumulating counters for a certain class
c     'END' to end/interrupt accumulating counters for a certain class
c     'FIN' to print the performance statistics
c The timing categories are defined by the user in the data statement below.
c Only one category can be active at a time
c NFLOP: number of floating point operations or communication operations
c The performance analysis is written to the file 'time.prc'
c If the timing routine timef is unavailable, it might be necessary to
c substitute it by another routine such as system_clock
C         written by S. Goedecker

      implicit real*8 (a-h,o-z)
      include 'mpif.h'
      character*6 category,cats
      character*3 action
      logical init
c set number NCAT of timing categories
      parameter(ncat=2)
      dimension cats(ncat),flops(ncat),timesum(ncat+1),
    1 wrktime(ncat+1),wrksquare(ncat),wrkflops(ncat),wrkflop2(ncat)
      save cats,time0,init,timesum,flops,total0

c define your performance categories (set NCAT to the corresponding value)
      data cats / 'SUMS', 'TRANSP' /
```

```
         if (action.eq.'INI') then

           do 11,i=1,ncat
c use appropriate timer to get time in seconds
           total0=timef()*1.d-3
           flops(i)=0.d0
11         timesum(i)=0.d0
           init=.false.

         else if (action.eq.'FIN') then

c sum results over all processor
c use appropriate timer to get time in seconds
           timesum(ncat+1)=timef()*1.d-3-total0
           if (nproc.gt.1) then
             call MPI_REDUCE(timesum,wrktime,ncat+1,
     1           MPI_DOUBLE_PRECISION,MPI_SUM,0,MPI_COMM_WORLD,ierr)
           else
             do 488,i=1,ncat+1
488          wrktime(i)=timesum(i)
           endif
           do 35,i=1,ncat
35         timesum(i)=timesum(i)**2
           if (nproc.gt.1) then
             call MPI_REDUCE(timesum,wrksquare,ncat,
     1           MPI_DOUBLE_PRECISION,MPI_SUM,0,MPI_COMM_WORLD,ierr)
             call MPI_REDUCE(flops,wrkflops,ncat,
     1           MPI_DOUBLE_PRECISION,MPI_SUM,0,MPI_COMM_WORLD,ierr)
           else
             do 124,i=1,ncat
             wrksquare(i)=timesum(i)
124          wrkflops(i)=flops(i)
           endif
           do 45,i=1,ncat
45         flops(i)=flops(i)**2
           if (nproc.gt.1) then
             call MPI_REDUCE(flops,wrkflop2,ncat,
     1           MPI_DOUBLE_PRECISION,MPI_SUM,0,MPI_COMM_WORLD,ierr)
           else
             do 874,i=1,ncat
874          wrkflop2(i)=flops(i)
           endif

           if (iproc.eq.0) then
             open(unit=60,file='time.prc',status='unknown')
             write(60,*)
     &'CATEGORY , TIME(sec) + dev , PERCENT ,   FLOPS + dev ,      SPEED
     &(Mflp)'
25           format(1x,a,2x,e10.3,e9.2,2x,f6.3,3x,e10.3,e9.2,2x,e10.3)
             sum=0.d0
             do 22,i=1,ncat
22           sum=sum+wrktime(i)
             do 20,i=1,ncat
             t1=wrktime(i)
             t2=sqrt(-t1**2+nproc*wrksquare(i))
             t3=wrktime(i)/sum
             t4=wrkflops(i)
```

```
                t5=sqrt(-t4**2+nproc*wrkflop2(i))
                t6=1.d-4*wrkflops(i)/wrktime(i)
20              write(60,25) cats(i),1.d-2*t1/nproc,1.d-2*t2/nproc,100.d0*t3,
         1           t4/nproc,t5/nproc,t6
                write(60,25) 'SUM  ',1.d-2*sum/nproc
                write(60,25) 'TOTAL',1.d-2*wrktime(ncat+1)/nproc
                write(60,*)  nproc,'processors'
                close(60)
              endif


          else


              do 100,i=1,ncat
              if (category.eq.cats(i)) then
              ii=i
              goto 200
              endif
100           continue
              print*, 'TIMING CATEGORY',category, ' NOT DEFINED'
              print*, 'ACTION  ',action
              stop 'TIMING CATEGORY NOT DEFINED'
200           continue


              if (action.eq.'STR') then
                if (init.neqv..false.) then
                    print*, cats(ii),': TIMING RESTARTED BEFORE ENDED'
                stop
                endif
c use appropriate timer to get time in seconds
                time0=timef()*1.d-3
                init=.true.
              else if (action.eq.'END') then
                if (init.neqv..true.) then
                      print*, cats(ii), ':NOT STARTED BEFORE ENDED'
                stop
                endif
                flops(ii)=flops(ii)+nflop
c use appropriate timer to get time in seconds
                timesum(ii)=timesum(ii)+timef()*1.d-3-time0
                init=.false.
              else
                stop 'TIMING ACTION UNDEFINED'
              endif


          endif


          end
```

A.3   Program that should run at peak speed

```
      program peak


      implicit real*8 (a-h,o-z)
      parameter(nexp=14,nn=2**nexp,nrep=400)
      parameter(cyclehertz=120.d6)
      dimension
     &  time_sec(nexp),speed_Mflops(nexp),cycle(nexp)
      dimension v(4)



      do 100,il=0,nexp
      v(1)=1.d-26
      v(2)=1.d-26
      v(3)=1.d-26
      v(4)=1.d-26
      nl=2**il
      nit=nrep*(nn/nl)
C     t1=mclock()*1.d-2
      t1=second()
      do 10,it=1,nit
      call sub_1(nl,v(1),v(2),v(3),v(4))
10    continue
C     t2=mclock()*1.d-2
      t2=second()
      time_sec(il)=(t2-t1)
      nflops=32*nrep*nn
      speed_Mflops(il)=(nflops/time_sec(il))*1.d-6
      cycle(il)=time_sec(il)*cyclehertz/(nflops)
100   continue



      write(6,*) 'CYCLES, SPEED (MFLOPS), TIME (sec)'
      do il=0,nexp
21    format(1x,i2,1x,i9,f6.2,f8.1,e10.3)
      write(6,21) il,2**il,cycle(il),speed_Mflops(il),time_sec(il)
      enddo
      write(6,*) v


      end



      subroutine sub_1(n,x1,x2,x3,x4)
c ''normally'' written version, gives peak speed for instance on IBM POWER2
      implicit real*8 (a-h,o-z)
      do 10,i=1,n
      y1=x1 + .500007500110d-05*x2 + .100001500023d-04*x3
      y2=x2 + .500007500110d-05*x1 + .100001500023d-04*x4
      y3=x3 + .100001500023d-04*x1 + .500007500110d-05*x4
      y4=x4 + .100001500023d-04*x2 + .500007500110d-05*x3

      x1=y1 + .500007500110d-05*y2 + .100001500023d-04*y3
```

```fortran
      x2=y2 + .500007500110d-05*y1 + .100001500023d-04*y4
      x3=y3 + .100001500023d-04*y1 + .500007500110d-05*y4
      x4=y4 + .100001500023d-04*y2 + .500007500110d-05*y3
10    continue


      return
      end



      subroutine sub_2(n,x1,x2,x3,x4)
c hand-optimized version also giving peak speed on SGI R10000
      implicit real*8 (a-h,o-z)
      do 10,i=1,n
      y1=x1 + .500007500110d-05*x2
      y2=x2 + .500007500110d-05*x1
      y3=x3 + .100001500023d-04*x1
      y4=x4 + .100001500023d-04*x2


      y1=y1 + .100001500023d-04*x3
      y2=y2 + .100001500023d-04*x4
      y3=y3 + .500007500110d-05*x4
      y4=y4 + .500007500110d-05*x3


      x1=y1 + .500007500110d-05*y2
      x2=y2 + .500007500110d-05*y1
      x3=y3 + .100001500023d-04*y1
      x4=y4 + .100001500023d-04*y2


      x1=x1 + .100001500023d-04*y3
      x2=x2 + .100001500023d-04*y4
      x3=x3 + .500007500110d-05*y4
      x4=x4 + .500007500110d-05*y3


10    continue


      return
      end



      subroutine sub_3(n,x1,x2,x3,x4)
c software pipelined by hand for EV6 and T3E processors,
c some 90 percent of peak speed was attained
      implicit real*8 (a-h,o-z)


      s1=.500007500110d-05*x2
      s2=.500007500110d-05*x1
      s3=.100001500023d-04*x1
      s4=.100001500023d-04*x2
      s5=.100001500023d-04*x3
```

```
      s6=.100001500023d-04*x4
      s7=.500007500110d-05*x4
      s8=.500007500110d-05*x3


      y1=x1 + s1
      y2=x2 + s2
      y3=x3 + s3
      y4=x4 + s4
      y1=y1 + s5
      y2=y2 + s6
      y3=y3 + s7
      y4=y4 + s8


      s1=.500007500110d-05*y2
      s2=.500007500110d-05*x1
      s3=.100001500023d-04*x1
      s4=.100001500023d-04*x2
      s5=.100001500023d-04*x3
      s6=.100001500023d-04*x4
      s7=.500007500110d-05*x4
      s8=.500007500110d-05*x3


      x1=y1 + s1
      s1=.500007500110d-05*x2
      x2=y2 + s2
      s2=.500007500110d-05*x1
      x3=y3 + s3
      s3=.100001500023d-04*x1
      x4=y4 + s4
      s4=.100001500023d-04*x2


      x1=x1 + s5
      s5=.100001500023d-04*x3
      x2=x2 + s6
      s6=.100001500023d-04*x4
      x3=x3 + s7
      s7=.500007500110d-05*x4
      x4=x4 + s7
      s8=.500007500110d-05*x3


      do 10,i=2,n-1


      y1=x1 + s1
      s1=.500007500110d-05*y2
      y2=x2 + s2
      s2=.500007500110d-05*y1
      y3=x3 + s3
      s3=.100001500023d-04*y1
      y4=x4 + s4
      s4=.100001500023d-04*y2
```

```
y1=y1 + s5
s5=.100001500023d-04*y3
y2=y2 + s6
s6=.100001500023d-04*y4
y3=y3 + s7
s7=.500007500110d-05*y4
y4=y4 + s8
s8=.500007500110d-05*y3


x1=y1 + s1
s1=.500007500110d-05*x2
x2=y2 + s2
s2=.500007500110d-05*x1
x3=y3 + s3
s3=.100001500023d-04*x1
x4=y4 + s4
s4=.100001500023d-04*x2


x1=x1 + s5
s5=.100001500023d-04*x3
x2=x2 + s6
s6=.100001500023d-04*x4
x3=x3 + s7
s7=.500007500110d-05*x4
x4=x4 + s8
s8=.500007500110d-05*x3


10      continue


y1=x1 + s1
s1=.500007500110d-05*y2
y2=x2 + s2
s2=.500007500110d-05*y1
y3=x3 + s3
s3=.100001500023d-04*y1
y4=x4 + s4
s4=.100001500023d-04*y2


y1=y1 + s5
s5=.100001500023d-04*y3
y2=y2 + s6
s6=.100001500023d-04*y4
y3=y3 + s7
s7=.500007500110d-05*y4
y4=y4 + s8
s8=.500007500110d-05*y3


x1=y1 + s1
x2=y2 + s2
x3=y3 + s3
```

```
      x4=y4 + s4
      x1=x1 + s5
      x2=x2 + s6
      x3=x3 + s7
      x4=x4 + s8


      return
      end
```

A.4 Program for memory testing

```
      program memory_test


      implicit real*8 (a-h,o-z)
      real*4 etime,tarray(2)
      logical thrash


c stride adjusted to avoid cache thrashing or not
      parameter(thrash=.false.)
c number of operation needed for good statistics
      parameter(noops=10 000 000)
c fraction of physical cache size we want to fill at least
      parameter(frac=.66d0)
c maximum size of data set
      parameter(nexp=19,nn=2**nexp)
c maximum number of memory access operation per subroutine call (=maximum
loop length)
      parameter(mexp=19)
c maximum stride
      parameter(jumpex=14)


c cache and tlb parameters
c IBM 590 (4-way assoc cache, 2-way assoc TLB)
       parameter(ncache_line=32,ncache_size=8192)
       parameter(ntlb_line=512,ntlb_size=131072)
c IBM 590 (peak 265 Mflops)
      parameter(cyclehertz=66.d6)


      dimension x(nn,1),jump_arr(0:jumpex),time_sec(mexp,0:jumpex),
     &          speed_Mflops(mexp,0:jumpex),cycle(mexp,0:jumpex)


      do 24,m=1,mexp
      do 24,j=0,jumpex
24    cycle(m,j)=-1.d0


c initialize data
      do 33,i=1,nn
33    x(i,1)=1.d0
```

```
      if (thrash) then
c jumps that will give cache thrashing
      do j=0,jumpex
      jump_arr(j)=2**j
      enddo


      else
c adjust jumps to avoid cash thrashing
      write(6,*) 'Adjusted jumps'
      write(6,*) 'j,2**j,nd,lotc,lott'
      do j=0,jumpex
      nd=2**j
100   continue
        call cache_par(ncache_line,ncache_size,nd,lotc)
        call cache_par(ntlb_line,ntlb_size,nd,lott)
c if we have frac of the physical cache and tlb size, we are satisfied
      if (lotc.ge.frac*ncache_size/ncache_line .and.
     &     lott.ge.frac*ntlb_size/ntlb_line) then
C     write(6,*) j,2**j,nd,lotc,lott
      jump_arr(j)=nd
      goto 200
      endif
      nd=nd+1
      goto 100
200   continue
      write(6,*) j,2**j,nd,lotc,lott
      enddo


      endif


11      format(a,i2,a,f6.3,4(a,f5.1),25(a,f5.1),a)
22      format(1x,i2,4x,15(1x,f6.1))
12      format(1x,i3,1x,i14,3x,4(f14.2))


c TESTING---------------------------------------------
      do 300,m=3,mexp
      mcop=int(frac*2**m)


      do 300,j=0,jumpex


      jump=jump_arr(j)
      if (float(jump)*float(mcop).le.float(nn)) then


      nrep=max(1,noops/mcop)
      if (j.eq.0) nrep=10*nrep
      if (j.eq.1) nrep=4*nrep
      t1=mclock()*1.d-2
      do 30,it=1,nrep
C       call subs(nn,mcop,jump,x,
C     &           1.d0,2.d0,3.d0,4.d0,5.d0,6.d0,7.d0,8.d0)
```

```
        call subl(nn,mcop,jump,x,t12,t34,t56,t78)
30      continue
      t2=mclock()*1.d-2
      time_sec(m,j)=(t2-t1)
      nflops=nrep*mcop
      if (time_sec(m,j).ne.0.d0)
     &    speed_Mflops(m,j)=(nflops/time_sec(m,j))*1.d-6
      cycle(m,j)=time_sec(m,j)*cyclehertz/(nflops)
      endif
300     continue

      write(6,*) 'MEMORY_TEST results'


      write(6,*) 'CYCLES'
      do m=4,mexp
      write(6,21) m,(cycle(m,j),j=0,min(13,jumpex))
      enddo
      do m=4,mexp
      write(6,22) m,(cycle(m,j),j=14,jumpex)
      enddo


      write(6,*) 'SPEED (MFLOPS)'
      do m=4,mexp
      write(6,12) m,2**m,speed_Mflops(m,0)
      enddo


      end



      subroutine subs(nn,n,jump,x,t1,t2,t3,t4,t5,t6,t7,t8)
      implicit real*8 (a-h,o-z)
      dimension x(nn)


      if (jump.eq.1) then
      do 15,i=1,n-8+1,8
      x(i+0)=t1
      x(i+1)=t2
      x(i+2)=t3
      x(i+3)=t4
      x(i+4)=t5
      x(i+5)=t6
      x(i+6)=t7
      x(i+7)=t8
15      continue
      else
      do 10,i=1,n*jump-8*jump+1,8*jump
      x(i+0*jump)=t1
      x(i+1*jump)=t2
      x(i+2*jump)=t3
      x(i+3*jump)=t4
      x(i+4*jump)=t5
      x(i+5*jump)=t6
```

```
      x(i+6*jump)=t7
      x(i+7*jump)=t8
10    continue
      endif


      return
      end



      subroutine subl(nn,n,jump,x,t12,t34,t56,t78)
      implicit real*8 (a-h,o-z)
      dimension x(nn)


      t12=0.d0
      t34=0.d0
      t56=0.d0
      t78=0.d0
      if (jump.eq.1) then
      do 15,i=1,n-8+1,8
      s1=x(i+0)
      s2=x(i+1)
      t12=t12+s1*s2
      s3=x(i+2)
      s4=x(i+3)
      t34=t34+s3*s4
      s5=x(i+4)
      s6=x(i+5)
      t56=t56+s5*s6
      s7=x(i+6)
      s8=x(i+7)
      t78=t78+s7*s8
15    continue
      else
      do 10,i=1,n*jump-8*jump+1,8*jump
      s1=x(i+0*jump)
      s2=x(i+1*jump)
      t12=t12+s1*s2
      s3=x(i+2*jump)
      s4=x(i+3*jump)
      t34=t34+s3*s4
      s5=x(i+4*jump)
      s6=x(i+5*jump)
      t56=t56+s5*s6
      s7=x(i+6*jump)
      s8=x(i+7*jump)
      t78=t78+s7*s8
10    continue
      endif


      return
      end
```

```
      subroutine subc(nn,n,jump,x,y)
      implicit real*8 (a-h,o-z)
      dimension x(n),y(n)


      if (jump.eq.1) then
      do 15,i=1,n-8+1,8
      x(i+0)=y(i+0)
      x(i+1)=y(i+1)
      x(i+2)=y(i+2)
      x(i+3)=y(i+3)
      x(i+4)=y(i+4)
      x(i+5)=y(i+5)
      x(i+6)=y(i+6)
      x(i+7)=y(i+7)
15    continue
      else
      do 10,i=1,n-8*jump+1,8*jump
      x(i+0*jump)=y(i+0*jump)
      x(i+1*jump)=y(i+1*jump)
      x(i+2*jump)=y(i+2*jump)
      x(i+3*jump)=y(i+3*jump)
      x(i+4*jump)=y(i+4*jump)
      x(i+5*jump)=y(i+5*jump)
      x(i+6*jump)=y(i+6*jump)
      x(i+7*jump)=y(i+7*jump)
10    continue
      endif


      return
      end
```

A.5   Program to test suitability of parallel computers for fine-grained tasks

```
      program grain_mpi

      implicit real*8 (a-h,o-z)
      include 'mpif.h'
      parameter(ntotal=2**24)

c initialize MPI
C        write(6,*) 'start mpi'
      call MPI_INIT(ierr)
      call MPI_COMM_RANK(MPI_COMM_WORLD,iproc,ierr)
      call MPI_COMM_SIZE(MPI_COMM_WORLD,nproc,ierr)
      if (iproc.eq.0) write(6,*) 'nproc=',nproc

      if (iproc.eq.0)
     &   write(6,*) 'the total workload is always the same, so on a
     &   perfect parallel machine the total time would be constant'

      nrep=1
```

```
       do 200,isub=1,15
       nrep=nrep*2
       ndat=ntotal/nrep

       t1=mclock()
       do 100,irep=1,nrep

       call MPI_BCAST(ndat,1,MPI_INTEGER,0,MPI_COMM_WORLD,ierr)

       tt=1.d0
       do 10,i=1,ndat
       tt=sqrt(tt+1.d-1)
10     continue

       call MPI_REDUCE(tt,ttsum,1,
     1      MPI_DOUBLE_PRECISION,MPI_SUM,0,MPI_COMM_WORLD,ierr)

100    continue
       t2=mclock()
       time=(t2-t1)/100.d0
       if (iproc.eq.0) then
       write(6,*) 'repetitions,total time(sec)',nrep,time
       endif
200    continue


       call MPI_FINALIZE(ierr)

       end
```

A.6   Unrolled CI loop structure

```
C   y[ ii1 ii2 jj1 jj2 ]    x[ ii1  i2 jj1  j2 ]
        do jj1=1,nstat-1

        do ii1=1,nstat-1-3,4
        do jj2=jj1+1,nstat
        jy=ijnd(jj1,jj2)
        do   j2=jj1+1,nstat
        jx=ijnd(jj1, j2)

        do ii2=ii1+0+1,nstat
        iy1=ijnd(ii1+0,ii2)
        t1 = y(iy1,jy)
        ix1=ijnd(ii1+0, ii1+2+1)
        do   i2=ii1+2+1,ii1+0+1,-1
        t1 = t1 + qq( i2,ii2, j2,jj2)*x(ix1,jx)
        ix1=ijnd(ii1+0, i2-1)
        enddo
        y(iy1,jy) = t1
        enddo

        do ii2=ii1+1+1,nstat
        iy2=ijnd(ii1+1,ii2)
```

```
t2 = y(iy2,jy)
ix2=ijnd(ii1+1, ii1+2+1)
do  i2=ii1+2+1,ii1+1+1,-1
t2 = t2 + qq( i2,ii2, j2,jj2)*x(ix2,jx)
ix2=ijnd(ii1+1, i2-1)
enddo
y(iy2,jy) = t2
enddo

do ii2=ii1+2+1,nstat
iy3=ijnd(ii1+2,ii2)
t3 = y(iy3,jy)
ix3=ijnd(ii1+2, ii1+2+1)
do  i2=ii1+2+1,ii1+2+1,-1
t3 = t3 + qq( i2,ii2, j2,jj2)*x(ix3,jx)
ix3=ijnd(ii1+2, i2-1)
enddo
y(iy3,jy) = t3
enddo

do ii2=ii1+0+1,ii1+2+1
iy1=ijnd(ii1+0,ii2)
t1 = y(iy1,jy)
ix1=ijnd(ii1+0, nstat)
do  i2=nstat,ii1+3+1,-1
t1 = t1 + qq( i2,ii2, j2,jj2)*x(ix1,jx)
ix1=ijnd(ii1+0, i2-1)
enddo
y(iy1,jy) = t1
enddo

do ii2=ii1+1+1,ii1+2+1
iy2=ijnd(ii1+1,ii2)
t2 = y(iy2,jy)
ix2=ijnd(ii1+1, nstat)
do  i2=nstat,ii1+3+1,-1
t2 = t2 + qq( i2,ii2, j2,jj2)*x(ix2,jx)
ix2=ijnd(ii1+1, i2-1)
enddo
y(iy2,jy) = t2
enddo

do ii2=ii1+2+1,ii1+2+1
iy3=ijnd(ii1+2,ii2)
t3 = y(iy3,jy)
ix3=ijnd(ii1+2, nstat)
do  i2=nstat,ii1+3+1,-1
t3 = t3 + qq( i2,ii2, j2,jj2)*x(ix3,jx)
ix3=ijnd(ii1+2, i2-1)
enddo
y(iy3,jy) = t3
enddo

do ii2=ii1+3+1,nstat
iy1=ijnd(ii1+0,ii2)
t1 = y(iy1+0,jy)
t2 = y(iy1+1,jy)
```

```
t3 = y(iy1+2,jy)
t4 = y(iy1+3,jy)
ix1=ijnd(ii1+0, nstat)
do  i2=nstat,ii1+3+1,-1
t1 = t1 + qq( i2,ii2, j2,jj2)*x(ix1+0,jx)
t2 = t2 + qq( i2,ii2, j2,jj2)*x(ix1+1,jx)
t3 = t3 + qq( i2,ii2, j2,jj2)*x(ix1+2,jx)
t4 = t4 + qq( i2,ii2, j2,jj2)*x(ix1+3,jx)
ix1=ijnd(ii1+0, i2-1)
enddo
y(iy1+0,jy) = t1
y(iy1+1,jy) = t2
y(iy1+2,jy) = t3
y(iy1+3,jy) = t4
enddo

enddo
enddo
enddo

do ii1=ii1,nstat-1
do jj2=jj1+1,nstat
jy=ijnd(jj1,jj2)
do  j2=jj1+1,nstat
jx=ijnd(jj1, j2)
do ii2=ii1+1,nstat
iy=ijnd(ii1,ii2)
t1 = y(iy,jy)
ix=ijnd(ii1, nstat)
do  i2=nstat,ii1+1,-1
t1 = t1 + qq( i2,ii2, j2,jj2)*x(ix,jx)
ix=ijnd(ii1, i2-1)
enddo
y(iy,jy) = t1
enddo
enddo
enddo
enddo

enddo
```

Bibliography

[1] Jeanne C. Adams, ed., *Fortran* 95 *Handbook*, Scientific and Engineering Computation Series, Intertext Publications, McGraw-Hill, New York, 1997.

[2] R. Agarwal, B. Alpern, L. Carter, F. Gustavson, D. Klepacki, R. Lawrence, and M. Zubair, *High-performance parallel implementations of the NAS kernel benchmarks on the IBM SP2*, IBM Systems J., 34 (1995), p. 261.

[3] R. C. Agarwal, F. G. Gustavson, and M. Zubair, *Exploiting functional parallelism of POWER2 to design high-performance numerical algorithms*, IBM J. Res. Develop., 38 (1994), pp. 265.

[4] C. B. Stunket et al., *The SP2 high-performance switch*, IBM Systems J., 34 (1995), pp. 185–204.

[5] A. Aho, R. Sethi, and J. Ullman, *Compilers*, Addison-Wesley, Reading, MA, 1986.

[6] G. Almasi and A. Gottlieb, *Highly Parallel Computing*, 2nd ed., Benjamin/Cummings, Redwood City, CA, 1994.

[7] E. Anderson, Z. Bai, C. Bischof, J. Demmel, J. Dongarra, J. Du Croz, A. Greenbaum, S. Hammarling, A. McKenney, S. Ostrouchov, and D. Sorensen, *LAPACK Users' Guide*, 2nd ed., SIAM, Philadelphia, PA, 1995.

[8] R. Blainey, *Instruction scheduling in the TOBEY compiler*, IBM J. Res. Develop., 38 (1994), p. 577.

[9] D. Blickstein et al., *The GEM optimizing compiler system*, Digital Tech. J., 4 (1992), p. 121.

[10] W. L. Briggs, V. E. Henson, and S. F. McCormick, *A Multigrid Tutorial*, 2nd ed., SIAM, Philadelphia, PA, 2000.

[11] D. Culler and J. P. Singh, *Parallel Computer Architecture: A Hardware/Software Approach*, Morgan Kauffmann, San Francisco, 1998.

[12] J. J. Dongarra, I. S. Duff, D. C. Sorensen, and H. A. van der Vorst, *Numerical Linear Algebra for High-Performance Computers*, SIAM, Philadelphia, PA, 1998.

[13] K. Farkas, N. Jouppi, and P. Chow, *How Useful Are Non-blocking Loads, Stream Buffers, and Speculative Execution in Multiple Issue Processors*, WRL Research Report 8, Western Research Laboratory, Palo Alto, CA, 1994.

[14] A. Geist, A. Beguelin, J. Dongarra, W. Jiang, R. Manchek, and V. Sunderam, *PVM: Parallel Virtual Machine*, MIT Press, Cambridge, MA, 1994.

[15] S. Goedecker, *Fast radix 2, 3, 4, and 5 kernels for fast Fourier transformations on computers with overlapping multiply-add instructions*, SIAM J. Sci. Comput., 18 (1997), pp. 1605–1611.

[16] S. Goedecker, *Rotating a three-dimensional array in optimal positions for vector processing: Case study for a three-dimensional fast Fourier transform*, Comput. Phys. Comm., 76 (1993), p. 294.

[17] J. L. Hennessy and D. A. Patterson, *Computer Architecture, A Quantitative Approach*, Morgan Kauffmann, San Francisco, 1997.

[18] A. Hoisie, O. Lubeck, and H. Wasserman, *Performance and scalability analysis of teraflop-scale parallel architectures using multidimensional wavefront algorithms*, Int. J. High-Performance Comput. Appl., 14 (2000), p. 330.

[19] J. Hutter and T. Deutsch, *Personal communication*, 2000. hutter@oci.unizh.ch, Thierry.Deutsch@cea.fr.

[20] IEEE Comput., vol. 29, #12, Dec. 1996. Special issue.

[21] N. Jouppi, *Cache Write Policies and Performance*, WRL Research Report 12, Western Research Laboratory, Palo Alto, CA, 1991.

[22] F. T. Leighton, *Introduction to parallel algorithms and architecture: Arrays, trees, hypercubes*, Morgan Kauffmann, San Matteo, CA, 1996.

[23] J. M. Levesque and J. W. Williamson, *A Guidebook to Fortran on Supercomputers*, Academic Press, San Diego, CA, 1989.

[24] D. A. Patterson and J. L. Hennesey, *Computer Organization and Design*, Morgan Kaufmann, San Francisco, 1998.

[25] W. Press, B. P. Flannery, S. A. Teukolsky, and W. T. Vetterling, *Numerical Recipes, The Art of Scientific Computing*, Cambridge University Press, Cambridge, UK, 1986. (Supplementary information available online at http://www.nr.com.)

[26] M. Quinn, *Parallel Computing*, McGraw-Hill, New York, 1994.

[27] V. Sarkar, *Automatic selection of high-order transformations in the IBM XL FORTRAN compilers*, IBM J. Res. Develop., 41 (1997), p. 233.

[28] M. Snit, S. Otto, S. Huss-Lederman, D. Walker, and J. Dongarra, *MPI: The complete reference*, MIT Press, Cambridge, MA, 1996 and W. Gropp, E. Lusk, and A. Skjelluj, *Using MPI*, MIT Press, Cambridge, MA, 1994.

[29] C. Van Loan, *Computational Frameworks for the Fast Fourier Transform*, SIAM, Philadelphia, PA, 1992.

[30] P. H. Worley, *The effect of time constraints on scaled speedup*, SIAM J. Sci. Statist. Comput., 11 (1990), pp. 838–858.

Index